Routedge Revivals

Mary Kingsley

The name of Mary Kingsley deserves to be more widely known than it is today. A woman of rare abilities and boundless courage, living in an age when the narrowest Victorian conventions about the duties of daughters in the home still prevailed, she nevertheless achieved fame and distinction as a traveller in the wildest regions of West Africa, a writer, an ethnologist, and an expert on Colonial Government.

As a young woman, Mary Kingsley had no life beyond the strict confines of her home; not until 1892, when she was thirty, did freedom come to her. Instantly this astonishing young woman began the work, which was to lead her to remote, unexplored regions of 'the Coast'. Along unmapped rivers, to a study of cannibals, and in England, to a political struggle to which she wholeheartedly gave herself for the welfare of the peoples of West Africa, until her death in 1900.

In vivid, discursive travel books, Mary Kingsley described her experiences with immense detachment and humour. These lengthy works have long been out of print, but in *Mary Kingsley: A Victorian in the Jungle* (first published in 1957) Olwen Campbell, by presenting selected extracts, preserves in a concise form the record of these strange adventures. But the adventures themselves are only a part of a remarkable life story. The effects on Mary Kingsley's character of her oppressive home life are fully brought out for the first time, and some explanation is suggested of a most enigmatic personality. Fresh light is also thrown on her political work, and her character, by a number of extracts from a series of remarkable letters, never before published.

Mary Kingsley
A Victorian in the Jungle

Olwen Campbell

First published in 1957
by Methuen & Co Ltd

This edition first published in 2024 by Routledge
4 Park Square, Milton Park, Abingdon, Oxon, OX14 4RN

and by Routledge
605 Third Avenue, New York, NY 10017

Routledge is an imprint of the Taylor & Francis Group, an informa business

© 1957 Olwen Campbell

All rights reserved. No part of this book may be reprinted or reproduced or utilised in any form or by any electronic, mechanical, or other means, now known or hereafter invented, including photocopying and recording, or in any information storage or retrieval system, without permission in writing from the publishers.

Publisher's Note
The publisher has gone to great lengths to ensure the quality of this reprint but points out that some imperfections in the original copies may be apparent.

Disclaimer
The publisher has made every effort to trace copyright holders and welcomes correspondence from those they have been unable to contact.

A Library of Congress record exists under LCCN: 58000825

ISBN: 978-1-032-83393-4 (hbk)
ISBN: 978-1-003-50912-7 (ebk)
ISBN: 978-1-032-83395-8 (pbk)

Book DOI 10.4324/9781003509127

Mary Kingsley, aged thirty-four

MARY KINGSLEY
A Victorian in the Jungle

by

OLWEN CAMPBELL

METHUEN & CO LTD
36 ESSEX STREET · LONDON WC2

First published in 1957

CATALOGUE NUMBER 6014/U

PRINTED IN GREAT BRITAIN BY
BUTLER AND TANNER LTD, FROME AND LONDON

TO
MY DAUGHTERS
LAURA AND CLARE

Contents

Preface	*page* 9
PART I: HEREDITY AND ENVIRONMENT	
1. Early Years	13
PART II: EIGHT YEARS OF ACHIEVEMENT	
2. The First Journey	35
3. The Second Journey: The Rivers	61
4. The Second Journey: 'Going for Bush'	82
5. Some Animals and a Mountain	102
6. The 'Mind Forest'	120
7. The Forest of Politics	137
8. Books and Friends	158
9. The Last Job	173
Notes and References	187
Bibliography	192
Index	193

Illustrations

Mary Kingsley, aged thirty-four	*frontispiece*
Trading canoe at Sette Cama, French Congo, 1899	*facing page* 49
Dug-out canoe, French Congo	64
Kabendas from South Congo	64
Canoe and jungle, Lagos Creeks	97
Peaks of Cameroons mountain (from Burton's *Abeokuta and the Camaroons Mountains*, 1863)	112
Cameroons mountain in eruption, 1954	112
Mary Kingsley, in 1896 or 1897	144
John Holt, *c.* 1900	161
Fishing canoe and beach, near Victoria	176
Map—The Second Journey	*page* 34

(*Permission to reproduce illustrations has been kindly given by Mr. C. R. Holt, the Shell Petroleum Company, and West African Newspapers Limited.*)

Preface

The reasons which determined me to write this biography were many and various. In the first place there was the inducement of a keen admiration and liking for Mary Kingsley's character and a desire to throw fresh light on her strange personality. I had read Stephen Gwynn's life of her with great enjoyment, but it has some serious defects and, like Mary's own travel books, it is now not only out of print but almost unobtainable. It seemed that there was room for another biography, and while I was hesitating a lot of new material came into my hands.

Stephen Gwynn, whose *Life of Mary Kingsley* was published in 1932, had known her well and greatly admired her. He was able to provide much information, some of it from sources now no longer available. His book will remain the standard work on its subject and it is indispensable to any subsequent biographer. But though it is full of interest and charm it takes little account of the influence on her character of her early life; and its mass of material seems to have been thrown together in some disorder, so that the reader is left with a confused recollection of comment, information and fascinating anecdote scattered about at random. The unreliable index of the first edition does little to help him, while the second edition has no index, and prints new material of different dates collected together into a final Postscript.

Our knowledge of Mary's childhood and of her travels comes almost entirely from her own writings. Until her books

Preface

—*Travels in West Africa* and *West African Studies*—are re-issued, in whole or shortened versions, a biographer, by quoting at length from her masterly descriptions of her adventures, can help to keep alive the memory of books which ought to be a permanent part of our literary heritage instead of lying forgotten on the shelves of a few public libraries.

When, after her second journey, Miss Kingsley became famous she made numerous friends and wrote a great number of letters, most of them on political affairs connected with West Africa. I have been very fortunate in being lent by Mr C. R. Holt of Liverpool, copies of the unpublished letters—over a hundred—written by Mary to his grandfather John Holt between 1897 and 1900. I am deeply indebted to Mr Holt for his kindness in allowing me to quote from these letters, and for the infinite trouble he has taken in giving me information and advice. Future students of West African history may owe much to the firm of John Holt and Company for the care with which they have preserved over several generations their interesting African records.

Mr Holt has also allowed me to quote from letters written to his grandfather by Mrs J. R. Green, Mary Slessor and others after Mary Kingsley's death.

I have to thank Mr Charles Johnson for permission to read and use some very entertaining letters of Mary's to his aunt, Miss H. Johnson; and to the Women's Service Library for the loan of the rough notes from which Miss Kingsley delivered a vigorous speech opposing Women's Suffrage.

Mary Kingsley's papers, including presumably her travel diaries, passed at her death to her brother Charles George. He survived her by only nine years, during which he got no further than preparing to write a life of his sister. 'In course of time', Gwynn rather cryptically remarks, 'her papers perished accidentally where they were stored.'

PART I

HEREDITY AND ENVIRONMENT

I

Early Years

Mary Kingsley ought not to be forgotten. In her character and adventures she was quite unlike anyone who had ever existed before.

She was born in 1862, and died in 1900 at the age of thirty-eight. The first thirty years of her life were passed in almost total seclusion, her strong personality and eager mind imprisoned in a narrow domestic life and burdened with the care of a delicate mother. When both her parents died early in 1892 she quickly became famous and indeed notorious. She explored alone some of the wildest parts of West Africa, making friends with cannibals, collecting zoological specimens and studying tribal customs; coming home full of new ideas about colonial government, to deliver lectures up and down the country and write articles and two fat books of a very original and provocative kind. The large crowds who heard her lectures were fascinated by her peculiar mixture of earnestness and impish humour, of humility and hard-hitting exhortation, and politicians and administrators turned to her for information and advice. She soon became an important figure in colonial government circles and scientific societies. She made many friends and wrote hundreds of letters, mostly concerned with the welfare of her beloved West Africa. Her two books of travel and ethnology were best-sellers. When the Boer War came she felt reluctantly that it was South Africa, not West,

Heredity and Environment

which needed her. She went out early in 1900 and was given the job of nursing Boer prisoners. After three months of work almost as grim as that which Florence Nightingale did in Scutari, she succumbed to enteric fever, and was buried at sea. The swirling waters of the twentieth century soon closed over her. She would not have minded: she had striven to serve, not to be remembered; her own life was light weight to her. She said of herself: 'I am no more a human being than a gust of wind is . . . I have never had a human individual life; I have always been the doer of odd jobs and lived in the joys, sorrows and worries of other people.'[1]

But these are the words after all of a very individual and remarkable person; and we cannot afford to let her go with the wind.

There are reasons for the comparative obscurity into which Mary Kingsley has fallen. In the first place, though her influence on British colonial policy may have been great, it is not a thing that can be measured. Her lectures roused public interest in the colonies, and for a time changed the climate of opinion in regard to Africa. She strengthened enlightened policies by her articles and by private talks and communications with the leading men of the Colonial Office: Mr Joseph Chamberlain constantly sought her advice—though he did not always take it. And if she were alive today it is possible that she would maintain that a wrong attitude to native peoples and an ignorance of their customs and of the geography of the country were still creating trouble, involving us in loss of life and money; and many people would agree with her. On the other hand her boundless faith in the outstanding virtues and claims to leadership of the British nation would be generally regarded today as almost indecent.

Her two books—*Travels in West Africa* and *West African Studies*—have long been out of print, and are only accessible in libraries. And when you get hold of them it is difficult to

Early Years

know how to take them. Their five or six hundred pages of close print run on through brilliant descriptions, strange adventures, comic anecdotes, ethnological research, comprehensive study of native religions, and the history of African trade; and these many ingredients are so inter-mixed that you never know from page to page whether you will be listening to a treatise on Fetish or to a Thurberesque misadventure.

Then again the very queerness of the adventures into which this dare-devil traveller constantly stumbled might lead to a certain amount of disbelief, a disbelief wholly unwarranted (for she had a scrupulous regard for truth), but encouraged by the comic and slightly flippant manner in which she relates many of her experiences.

As a character she may have suffered in rather the same way—seeming at first sight too strange to be real. We may feel for a moment as the countryman did who saw his first giraffe at the zoo and remarked: 'Them things don't exist.' How could a Victorian lady, brought up in domestic seclusion and possessing so much of the diffidence and modesty, the tender-heartedness and self-abnegation of her sex and period, be also a madly fearless explorer, singularly immune to horrors, and a thumper of political tubs? She did much of her exploring in a voluminous Victorian dress, and delivered challenging and often rather slangy lectures clad in a curious old-fashioned hat. According to Sir George Goldie, the head of the Royal Niger Company, 'she had the brain of a man and the heart of a woman'. She had an inexhaustible fund of humour, but it sprang from depths of melancholy. Nearly all those who came in contact with her found her very lovable; but she remained all her life intensely lonely.

Fortunately no human individual can really be explained; but it could be held that a very paradoxical character is oftener made than born. The fascinating enigma of Mary Kingsley can best be understood from a study not only of

Heredity and Environment

her heredity but of the impact upon it of a very unusual environment.

Mary Kingsley was very proud of her ancestry—of the long line of fighting, seafaring, sporting Kingsleys whose records could be traced back for 600 years. A General Kingsley was an aide-de-camp at the Battle of Minden, a great-grandfather Lucas took part in important naval battles in the early years of the French Revolution. The Lucas family to which her father's mother belonged were a West Indian family settled there for six generations as planters, and at one time as slave-owners—a fact Mary reveals without embarrassment. She saw them, along with the fighting Kingsleys, as helping in the manner of their time to found the fortunes of the British Empire. 'I owe all that is good in me', she said at the end of her last lecture, 'to the blood of my ancestors.' [2] Her uncle, Charles Kingsley, at the height of his fame in 1865, wrote to Galton who was investigating the Kingsley stock for a book on heredity: 'We are but the *disjecta membra* of a most remarkable pair of parents. Our talent, such as it is, is altogether hereditary.' The close bonds of the family and its prevailingly masculine traditions down the generations expressed themselves with the recurring names of Charles and George and Henry, George Henry and Charles George; compromising for the daughters of the last two generations with Charlotte and Mary Henrietta. But though Mary Henrietta admired this tradition, she was not altogether uncritical. 'The family', she remarks in her Memoir of her father, had not been given 'to exhausting itself with rapidly successive outbreaks of intellectual brilliancy.' [3] It was the generation to which her uncles Charles and Henry and her father George belonged which seemed to her to constitute the 'Elizabethan period' of the clan.

The claim seems just, as the Rev. Chas. Kingsley, for some time rector of Clovelly, had remarkable offspring. Of his six children Charles became famous as a writer, philanthropist and

Early Years

preacher; Henry, the youngest, wrote novels, which were outstanding in his own time and are still read, notably *Ravenshoe*. George wrote many articles on natural history, and was part-author of a successful travel book, and in the rear of this battalion of male talent the one daughter, Charlotte, also wrote.

Charles and George were, after the death of an infant brother, the closest in age, and there was a great friendship between them, which survived into later life in spite of profound differences over religious matters. The eldest of the whole family, Gerald, had died nearly twenty years before Mary was born, but he must be mentioned for the influence his tragic story may well have had on her childish mind.

'In 1844', Mary writes, 'he met with a ghastly death in the Gulf of Carpentaria on board a disease-stricken gun-boat... she lay with her wretched crew rotting and pining... never heard of nor hearing of a living soul outside for a year and a half.'[4] Finally no officer was left except Gerald who stuck to his post and kept the ship, as ordered, at her station, till he died himself. One cannot help feeling that on Mary's ardent mind this story may have acted as something of a challenge; and she will have been mindful of this uncle when she chose to visit the most disease-ridden districts of West Africa.

But though this 'Elizabethan' generation were inspired by the Kingsley traditions of adventurousness and toughness, they were most of them anything but tough and few of them enjoyed the normal span of life. Perhaps indeed they did, to use Mary's phrase, exhaust themselves with intellectual brilliance. One thinks of Charles Kingsley as the sporting parson, nicknamed 'muscular Christian', but he was in fact a hypersensitive, nervous and delicate man, who died from recurrent chest affections at the age of fifty-six. George, Mary's father, was the toughest, and Mary thinks the happiest, of the group, but he suffered towards the end of his life from

Heredity and Environment

rheumatic fever and heart weakness and died at sixty-six. Henry lived to be only forty-six. The wretched health which descended on him when he was quite a young man, warred with his thirst for adventure. He was at different times a gold digger, a stock rider, a miner and a mounted policeman, and in 1870 a war correspondent with the German army. When he turned to novel writing he wrote so well that it is rumoured his literary talent discouraged Charles. But by none of these methods did he succeed in making a comfortable income, and he lived to some extent on the generosity of his brothers.

Apart from the toughness which unfortunately was not handed down and the spirit of reckless adventure which continued undiminished and indeed reached its height in Mary and her father, there were other family characteristics which can be clearly seen through the four last generations. In the letter to Galton already quoted, Charles Kingsley wrote: 'My father was a magnificent man in body and mind, and was said to possess every talent except that of using them.' This trait appears again in both Henry and George. Of Henry, Mary says: 'All his life long he seemed to those who loved him to squander alike brilliant talents and brilliant opportunities without attaining happiness.' [5]

His elder brother George squandered his gifts in very much the same way, with one great difference—that he thoroughly enjoyed himself, at whatever cost to his wife and family.

George's character and way of life provide so many clues to an understanding of his daughter that much more must be said about him in due course. He had only two children; Mary was the elder; a brother, Charles George, was two years younger. In Charles George the tendency to waste talents, or at any rate opportunities, for talents may have been lacking, reappears along with physical delicacy. He was given—unlike his sister—an expensive education, but he did nothing with it. He planned to write a Memoir of his father, but after seven

Early Years

years nothing had been done and Mary did it instead. After her death he spent nine years intending to write her life, but when he died in 1910 at the age of forty-six nothing was ready, and the records and papers he left ultimately disappeared.

To Mary came a better portion of the family inheritance; the delicacy in a lesser degree; the tendency to waste talents and opportunities not at all. She was provided with very few opportunities but she created them for herself. In many respects she resembled her grandmother Kingsley of whom Charles Kingsley said, contrasting her with his father, 'My mother on the contrary had a quite extraordinary practical and administrative power; and she combines with it, even at her advanced age (79), my father's passion for knowledge, and the sentiment and fancy of a young girl.' Practical and administrative ability Mary had in plenty, and a passion for knowledge. The intense love of nature which both her grandparents possessed and by which their children were, one might almost say, obsessed, was undiminished in the grand-daughter; Mary showed as well a deep humanity and an urge to human service which seems to have been lacking in any of the 'Elizabethan generation' with the notable exception of Charles.

Of Mary's mother, Mary Bailey, we know almost nothing. She may have been of rather humble origin and responsible for the broad accent which Mary somehow acquired. George Kingsley appeared to be very much attached to his wife, in spite of the fact that from 1862—two years after his marriage—he spent the greater part of every year travelling about and indulging in reckless adventures. He was a good letter writer, and seems to have corresponded with a number of ladies. His letters to his wife, though long and affectionate, were infrequent owing to his roaming life, and Mrs Kingsley was constantly anxious about her husband on whom she seems to have lavished most of her devotion. Mary writes of her mother: 'She was a lady whose extraordinary benevolence endeared her

Heredity and Environment

to every one who was fortunate enough to come within the circle of her friendship, and whose faculty for managing affairs of business enabled her to take from her husband's shoulders the burden of many of the petty cares of life.' [6] Mrs George Kingsley lived in great seclusion; suffering from neglect and constant anxiety about her husband she soon became physically delicate. She solaced her loneliness with pet animals and books. 'The only thing that ever tempted her to go about among her neighbours was to assist them when they were sick in mind, body or estate. So strongly marked a characteristic was this of our early home life that to this day I always feel I have no right to associate with people unless there is something the matter with them.' [7]

This is an extraordinary statement; it becomes comprehensible as we learn more of the environment in which Mary fought to preserve the characteristics she had so markedly inherited.

The chief cause of this unnatural environment was certainly Mary's father—whom none the less she adored. No open mind can fail to see with what selfish irresponsibility he treated his wife and family.

George Kingsley had distinguished himself as a medical student and might have risen high in his profession and earned a good income. As quite a young man he had fought a cholera outbreak in Wales with notable courage and devotion; and there were many occasions in his travels when he showed both medical ability and kindness of heart. He was an enthusiast for all branches of scientific knowledge, was early elected a member of the Linnaean Society, and throughout his life contributed papers to scientific journals. But he was interested in too many things, and partly for that reason contracted out of the exacting obligations of a medical practitioner. At twenty-four he became private physician to the Marquis of Aylesbury, and, as Mary says 'went on in that capacity with one great nobleman after

Early Years

another'. This easy life enabled him to plan works on all sorts of subjects, including the Elizabethan dramatists; but these, like his later anthropological studies, remained embryonic—he was too restless to settle down to anything. He snatched at whatever travel he could get, and soon after his marriage in 1860 opportunities offered for travelling about the world as private physician to various adventurous and sporting aristocrats. His longest association was with the Earl of Pembroke, with whom he produced a book of travels—*South Sea Bubbles, by the Earl and the Doctor*. The more he travelled the further he wanted to go; and because he wanted, he went. 'I always wander,' he said, 'and wander I will, as long as there is a fresh bit of the world to see.'

His wife and two children he left meanwhile in a small house in Southwood Lane, Highgate, and here they lived for sixteen years, Mrs Kingsley managing the business affairs, and 'taking from her husband's shoulders the petty cares of life'. He would return home for two or three months of the year, some years not at all. Each visit added to the specimens and curios which filled every room, and to the odd collection of books in his library—books which, unknown to him, were his daughter's chief source of education and entertainment. Sometimes, presumably in George's absence, Henry Kingsley took refuge in an attic of his brother's house in order to get on with his novels away from the noise of his own home in Kentish Town. He will have provided Mary with some excitement by his own tales of travel and adventure.

The house stood back from the road and was surrounded by trees, the long garden being backed by two disused lanes where stray cattle and, it was rumoured, burglars sometimes congregated. But the threat of burglars too was something Mrs Kingsley was able to 'manage' for she was known in the district to be a good shot with a revolver. For Mary these threats of invasion enlivened the domestic round. ' "There is something

Heredity and Environment

in the lane" was a war-cry to the little house which was attended to with energy, irrespective of the nature of that something or of the hour at which it occurred.' These derelict lanes Mary refers to as 'the sporting region'.

In George's absence the main interest for the household was in his occasional long letters. They might come from any part of the world and they recorded every kind of adventure in vivid and humorous manner. His chief passion and occupation was hunting, and the letters are full of catalogues of creatures killed. Like Tom Thurnall in Charles Kingsley's *Two Years Ago* (a character partly modelled on George), 'he shot everything from a hippopotamus to a humming bird'. In her Memoir of her father Mary tries lamely to defend this characteristic of a 'noble and honourable English gentleman', but she herself had no sympathy with it; on her own travels she never killed an animal if she could avoid it, and she took pains to protect the wild creatures in Africa from the attentions of the big-game hunters.

The volume entitled *Notes on Sport and Travel* which, with her Memoir, Mary published eight years after her father's death, contains a number of his sketches of life in wild places and extracts from letters, some of which are worth preserving for their close observation and comic descriptions of queer animals. Some of these passages must have helped to form Mary's own style and manner; one might instance an exquisitely amusing account of the behaviour of land crabs (originally contributed to *The Field*). There are also many vivid and enthusiastic descriptions of scenery. Mary says that her father was capable of loyal affections and gentleness, and there are a few passages in the letters where he seems for a moment to reveal this gentler nature. On one occasion he has been dreaming of an imaginary Utopia in one of the lovely islands he has visited, and breaks off with: 'Yes!, this *is* sentimental. But you should never turn a sentiment away from your door. Take them all in—good, bad, and indifferent, and make the best of

Early Years

them, for maybe, if you slam the door in the face of one she'll never come again.' One likes him for saying this, yet one is forced almost at once to reflect how persistently he himself slammed the door on the most natural human sentiments and obligations.

The more irresponsible George was, the more responsible his little daughter had to be. In the few personal passages of the Memoir of her father—passages which are the main source of our knowledge of her childhood—she expresses deep devotion and admiration for him, but she was too clear-sighted to conceal the effects of his self-willed way of life. She had a vast sympathy for his love of adventure but she saw what the reckless indulgence of this love cost to others. The excuse she finds for him is charming; it is also amusing—and it is pathetic.

'I confess', she says, 'that in the old days I used to contemplate with a feeling of irritation the way in which my father used to reconcile and explain it to himself, that because he had a wife and family it was his dire and awful duty to go and hunt grizzly bears in a Red Indian infested district, and the like. I fancy now that I was wrong to have felt any irritation with him. It is undoubtedly true that he could have made more money had he settled down to an English practice as a physician; also undoubtedly true that he thoroughly enjoyed grizzly bear hunting and "loved the bright eyes of danger"; still there was in him enough of the natural man to give him the instinctive feeling that the duty of a father of a family was to go out hunting and fighting while his wife kept the home. But I am fully convinced that his taking this view of life really caused the illness which killed my mother. For months at a time she was kept in an unbroken strain of anxiety about him.' [8]

Her mother's delicacy increasingly darkened and restricted Mary's own life. But she was in any case brought up from the first for domesticity.

Heredity and Environment

'I was my mother's chief officer from the day I could first carry a duster, and I had to do the tidying up—that is to say, I became responsible for everything lost in the establishment.' This must have been something of an infliction on a high-spirited child; much worse was the fact that she was given almost no education, either because her father's way of life deprived his family of spare funds, or because both parents accepted the Victorian conception of woman's 'place' and functions. It is certainly remarkable that at a time when Charles Kingsley was campaigning in his books and public activities for the wider education of women, his niece, by far the most brilliant of her generation of Kingsleys, was left untaught. Near the end of her life she wrote in a letter to her publisher and friend, George Macmillan: 'I don't know if I ever revealed the fact to you that being allowed to learn German was *all* the paid-for education I ever had. £2000 was spent on my brother's, I still hope not in vain.' [9] The passage betrays some resentment, but on the whole she showed very little, although all her life she suffered from a certain diffidence and insecurity owing to her lack of educational grounding. She seems indeed to have accepted the view that men must travel while women must dust, and almost appeared to regard her own ultimate departure from pattern with a certain deprecating surprise, blaming her Kingsley blood for it, and presenting herself sometimes ruefully and sometimes rather gleefully as something of a freak.

Her parents were obviously unaware of her gifts, or indifferent to them. She devoted the best years of her young life to nursing her mother, and one assumes that there must have been a close affection between them, yet Mrs Kingsley seems never to have troubled to provide her daughter either with education or society. Though both Mary's travel books are dedicated to her brother Charles and there are many references in her letters to the duty of looking after him, she never

Early Years

mentions him as a playfellow when they were children or as a companion in later years.

It was to her father that she had to look for every stirring breath of the outer world. His adventures, his hair-breadth escapes, his glowing descriptions of wild and beautiful places, his close observations of nature, his scientific knowledge—here for Mary was life; and it is no wonder that she loved him. When he came home for a visit the sad, quiet little household was roused to intense if uncomfortable existence. George's 'awful temper' had been a byword among his brothers from boyhood, and his little daughter, who was so unsuitably and unpredictably enterprising in any field that offered, was bound to come into collision with him. She admits that she was provoking. Her responsibility for finding anything that was lost in the establishment 'embroiled' her with her father. So did her habit of carrying off some scientific book which he might be wanting himself. And she was liable to cause noises—her fighting cocks would crow too loud; and on one occasion, she relates, she experimented with gunpowder, and blew 'a tubful of liquid manure over the great spring blanket wash.... I had other reasons than scientific ones given me to remember that affair.'

But she could console herself with the reflection that however angry her father might sometimes be with her, he was made much angrier by Mr Gladstone's speeches, and would tear to shreds before the rest of the family had read it any paper which reported them. The awful temper certainly provided excitement, as well as exercises in diplomacy.

'It was not awful when you lived with it at close quarters and got used to it. It was volcanic, but never vindictive. I knew as a child perfectly well that if I successfully dodged a copy of Brand's *Dictionary of the Arts and Sciences*, or some other work, temporarily diverted into use as a projectile in consequence

Heredity and Environment

of some conduct of mine, all would be well, provided I went away and was quiet for a time. No one in his family knew half so much of his temper as I did. His wife he was ever anxious about on account of her delicate health; moreover, she was not an irritating person to anyone—neither was his son; but I was so mainly because in early years I was liable, either directly or indirectly, to cause sudden noises. For example, I had in early life a taste for fighting cocks; my mother, who was fond of any kind of animal let me keep them. During those long months when my father was absent from home those fighting cocks behaved well; when he came home they did little else but crow. There is something fine in a gamecock's crow, and it is stirring: it used to produce that effect on my father considerably, and I might just as well have crowed those crows myself, for I was held accountable for them.' [10]

These cocks were never allowed by their mistress to fight each other, so they had a suppressed longing for battle; George Kingsley, who resented their crowing, used to be highly amused when they attacked the postman and drove him into the coal cellar; yet Mary was blamed if they annoyed the neighbours. It all seemed to her very unfair.

Yet deprived and frustrated as she was, it is plain that she was never cowed. Since education, for which she longed, was not provided, she provided it for herself as well as she could, in spite of parental disapproval of her choice of subjects. But that choice was dictated after all by what she could find in her father's library—and a very odd collection of books she read. In an account of her early life written in 1899 for the journal *Mainly About People* she tells the story of her efforts at self-education.

'The whole of my childhood and youth was spent at home, in the house and garden. The living outside world I saw little of, and cared less for, for I felt myself out of place at the few

Early Years

parties I ever had the chance of going to, and I deservedly was unpopular with my own generation, for I knew nothing of play and such things. But this was not superiority of mind in me, at all; the truth was I had a great amusing world of my own other people did not know, or care about—that was in the books in my father's library.

'They were mostly old books on the West Indies, and old medical books, and old travel books and what not; fiction was represented in it by the works of Smollett, and little else. No one would believe the number, or character, of the books I absorbed. I did not say anything about them, finding if I did it generally meant an injunction not to do it. My favourites among them were Burton's *Anatomy of Melancholy*, Johnson's *Robberies and Murders of the Most Notorious Pirates*, and Bayle's *Dictionary*. When my father was home from one of his long and many journeys, new books used to come into the house, and although I did not like them as the old, yet they had to be read too. But just as I was coming to the conclusion that new books were unworthy of my serious attention, one turned up that fascinated me wildly. It was *Solar Physics*, by Professor Norman Lockyer. That book opened a new world for me, and also got me into trouble in my old one.

'It was difficult to get hold of, because my father was interested in it, too, but still I stuck to it, and one dreadful evening my father's friend, the doctor, came in. My father asked him if he had read *Solar Physics*, said it was an interesting book, etc., and finally, that he would lend it him and send it round in the morning. I thought, "No, not if I know it will you lend that book", and so I took it and hid it away in some straw in a shed.

'I need not say when a search for it next morning was instituted I was held to know where it was. I said neither aye nor nay, and the book returned to civilised society when I had got right through it—not before.

Heredity and Environment

'About this time I developed a passionate devotion for the science of chemistry, and I went in for it—experiments not being allowed—in the available books in the library. Most of them were books on alchemy, and the rest entirely obsolete. After most carefully getting up all the information these could give me, I happened on a gentleman who knew modern chemistry, and tried my information on him. He said he had not heard anything so ridiculous for years, and recommended I should be placed in a museum as a compendium of exploded chemical theories, which hurt my feelings very much, and I cried bitterly at not being taught things.

'My home authorities said I had no business to want to be taught such things, but presented me with a copy of Craik's *Pursuit of Knowledge Under Difficulties*.' [11]

Her life, she later says, including her African travels, could be summed up as 'doing odd jobs and trying to understand things, pursuing knowledge under difficulties with unbroken devotion'.

She tried to learn some mathematics, and accumulated enough money to 'take in that delightful paper *The English Mechanic*; what *The English Mechanic* was to me for years I cannot explain. What I should have done without its companionship between sixteen and twenty I do not care to think. We had at this period of my existence moved down into northwest Kent, to a secluded spot where the houses were always in some state of dilapidation, where the residents had to be handy men if they would not lead miserable existences. I became a handy man.'

The odd assortment of knowledge which this lonely girl acquired almost suggests some subconscious plotter at work equipping her for the future she can so little have foreseen.

By 1879 George Kingsley was beginning to relinquish his roaming life, and he moved with his family to Bexley Heath in

Early Years

the hope that the drier climate might benefit his wife's health. He may also have been concerned about his own tendency to rheumatism. Four years later when Mary was twenty-one they moved again, this time to Cambridge where Mary's brother Charles was entering college.

It must have been during this period that Mary became what she called her father's 'underworker', using for the purpose the only part of her educational equipment which had been provided for her.

She had been taught German, she says, so that she could do odd jobs for her father in looking up German authorities. His chief interest at this time was in anthropology, and Mary was charged with collecting accounts given by travellers of sacrificial rites. It was not a very lady-like job, and might one would think have been included among 'the things that she ought not to want to learn'! But her father found her most useful, and as she was well primed in the robberies and murders of the most notorious pirates, and many other blood-thirsty tales, we may feel sure she did not turn a hair; she merely acquired knowledge, and a degree of tolerance and sang-froid valuable for subsequent hob-nobbing with cannibals. She very much enjoyed this collaboration with her father, and the desire to continue his unfinished work was one reason she gave for her travels.

George Kingsley 'revelled' in Cambridge life, and delighted in meeting scholars and scientists; so too might Mary have done if circumstances had allowed. The shyness which had been encouraged by her isolated life would not have cut her off from making friends and finding fresh nourishment for her eager mind, but the load of home responsibility was steadily increasing as her mother grew iller, and soon her father's health too began to cause anxiety.

During the nine years that Mary lived in Cambridge the few who met her were attracted by the slim, pale girl with her straight fair hair, honest eyes and an insatiable interest in

Heredity and Environment

things of the mind, but hardly anyone was able to improve on the acquaintance, she was so constantly shut up at home. One young woman of about her own age did manage to break through the barrier; this was Violet Paget, a daughter of the physician Sir George Paget who was friendly with George Kingsley. Violet Paget, afterwards Mrs Roy, acquired a passionate and life-long affection for Mary, and from her we get some account of Mary's difficult life. She found that Mrs Kingsley was a cruelly exacting invalid, insisting that, day or night, only her daughter should wait on her. Just once Mary was persuaded to go with the Pagets for a short holiday in Wales, but no sooner had she arrived than she was summoned home by telegram.[12] Of these years Mary writes that they were 'years of work and watching and anxiety, a narrower life in home interests than ever, and a more hopelessly depressing one, for it was a losing fight with death all the time'.

Her parents died within a few weeks of each other early in 1892, her father from heart failure in his sleep, her mother after long suffering. A passage from a letter written in 1897 to a missionary friend who had raised the subject of religious faith, reveals how great was the strain which had been put upon her from childhood and how it had affected her spirit. She owns that she is liable to deep melancholy, and continues:

'Far under the melancholy there is an utter faith in God which I fear I could not make you believe I have. Nevertheless it is there, and it has survived my being educated among agnostics, and the dreadful gloom of all my life until I went to Africa. . . . I do not mean that my faith is any use except to the owner, or that it is comfortable and restful; for I have always a feeling of responsibility. All through the fifteen years during which I nursed my mother and watched over my brother's delicate health, I never felt "it was all for the best", but only that perhaps I could make things better for them—if only I knew

Early Years

how, or were more able; and I tried my best, and I know I failed, for my mother's sufferings were terrible, and my brother's health is still far from what I should wish.' [13]

In the summer of 1892 Mary's brother sailed for the Far East in search of health and recreation, and she was no longer needed at home. She was deeply grieved by the death of her parents and felt weary and broken-hearted, but she found herself possessed of a small income of £500 a year and the opportunity for the first time to realize an individual life. She was thirty years old.

PART II

EIGHT YEARS
OF ACHIEVEMENT

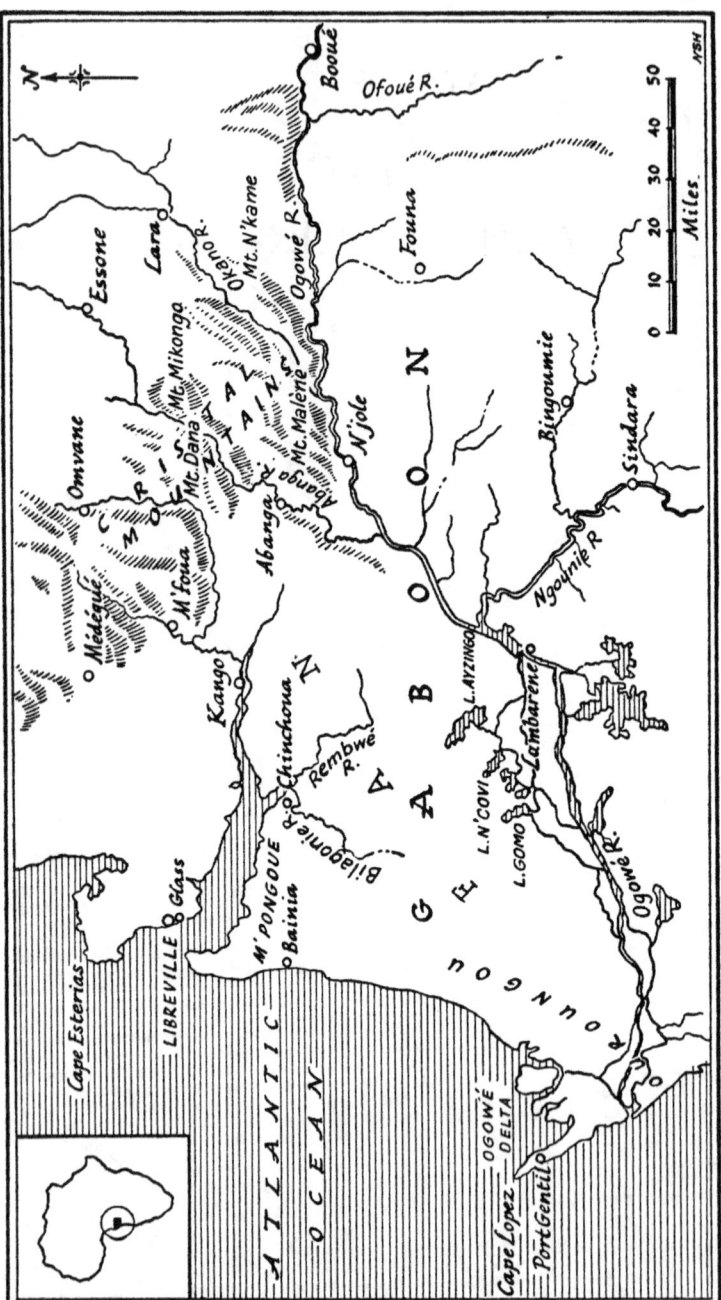

THE SECOND JOURNEY (See Chapters 3 & 4)

Based on the French Colonial Ministry's *Carte du Cameroun*, this map has certain names altered to Mary Kingsley's spelling. Her travels cannot be clearly indicated as much of the country she explored is still uncharted, and there is great variation in the names given to places on different maps today. Also, many of the villages now marked on maps did not exist in her time.

2

The First Journey

One turns with an enormous feeling of relief and pleasure to Mary's years of freedom—years which she packed so full of activity, adventure and public service, and some of which she so much enjoyed. What she called 'sky-larking in Africa', a sport which involved incredible discomforts as well as dangers, seems to have satisfied her nature as nothing else could have done. Here she found endless opportunities for exploring queer places and making queer friends, and for exercising her inexhaustible sense of humour and fun. The energies so long checked back, flowed out in a flood.

But the shadow of the past remained with her. It is common enough for a biographer to lament the loss the world suffers when highly gifted men and women are cut off by early death. We seldom mourn—perhaps we can seldomer see—the damage or destruction of rare qualities, the toll taken of personality, no matter how strong, by unnatural frustrations in youth. We forget that the spirit may lose a limb as the body can.

Everything that Mary Kingsley did and felt in the years of her freedom was coloured by the experiences of those early years during which so much of what belonged to her rich nature and heredity had been stifled by demands made and opportunities refused. She had been in a peculiar way *depersonalized*, and the loss is ours as well as hers. She had come to feel

Eight Years of Achievement

that she did not matter, and that feeling was bound to separate her to some extent from her friends, as it does from her biographer. Beneath her spontaneity and candour there was an iron barrier of reserve—a reserve which was probably quite unconscious, for she sometimes complained of loneliness and of not being understood. The origin of this reserve was perhaps a strongly suppressed resentment at the merciless way she had been exploited by the parents she had loved and served so faithfully; by the father she had so generously understood, but who had never troubled to understand her.

At the period of her young life when she had needed to discover and develop some of her own personal urges and ideals, constant and absorbing claims had been made on her time, her pity, and her sense of responsibility for others. Apart from this drain on her feelings, her emotional life was starved. She may well have been temperamentally shy and critical, but this tendency can only have been increased by such great isolation from normal human contacts outside her home. And though she was so much immersed in family life, there is nothing to suggest that any of her family on their side reached out in sympathy and understanding to her. 'Not one of my own people is interested in the smallest degree in what I do or think,' she said in a letter to John Holt in 1898; the 'own people' referred to here were not, apart from her brother, her immediate family, for her parents were long dead; but there is every reason for thinking that this had been the attitude to her from the first in her own family circle.

It is not surprising that when at last she achieved a full life, though she could give warm and loyal friendship she could not give herself; she was in some ways unapproachable; irretrievably self-dependent and emotionally alone. 'I have never been in love,' she once said, 'nor has anyone ever been in love with me.'

In her sketch of her own life she writes: 'My life has been

The First Journey

one wholly without romance or variety in the proper sense of the word.... Why this has been is perfectly clear; it arises from my having no personal individuality of my own whatsoever. I have always lived in the lives of other people, whose work was heavy for them; and apart from that I have lived a life of my own, strewn about among non-human things.'

A still greater degree of diffidence and aloofness appears in a later passage of the letter in which she said: 'I am no more a human being than a gust of wind is.' She continues:

'It never occurs to me that I have any right to do anything more than now and then sit and warm myself at the fires of real human beings. I am grateful to them for letting me do this. I am fond of them, but I don't expect them to be fond of me, and it is just as well I don't—for there is not one of them who has ever cared for me apart from my services.... I am no better than the human beings I deal with in the matter of feeling. When they are happy and comfortable and snug, I lose all interest in them—as well as they in me—it is quite mutual, save that I have more reason to be grateful to them than they to me, for it is through them I know this most amusing human world; but it is the non-human world I belong to myself.' [1]

We have to pick our way carefully among these strange confessions: they cannot be accepted literally. A life which held, even if only for a few years, such original adventures experienced with so much zest, and which was enriched by so many and varied friendships, can hardly be regarded as without romance and variety. Nor can we agree with her that she lacked individuality, since her individuality cries aloud in all that she did and wrote. When she implies that she had no human side, no real bonds with other people, she is being unjust to them and to herself. She was greatly loved by many

Eight Years of Achievement

people during those last years of her life; and the ardour with which she fought for wiser and juster treatment of Africans came from a very human, compassionate heart. Her remoteness was not due to lack of feeling.

After her death her friend, Mrs J. R. Green, wrote of her to John Holt: 'It is hard to tell the experience of that life in which every personal hope and fear had been laid aside, and nothing left but service to all who needed it. Its dark and solitary side, its profound obedience, could never be put into words.' [2]

Our understanding of the real Mary Kingsley is made difficult by her habit of presenting almost everything that happened to herself as though it were unimportant except in so far as it is funny. But no façade of self-mockery can conceal the greatness of her courage. It was a lonely courage—and was all the greater for that. She went out on her travels humbly, with no support from home or expectation of recognition. She faced fear and quite often terror, and exposed herself to danger again and again because the preservation of her own life had ceased to seem much worth bothering about; far more important, she felt, was to understand and help 'those poor "nigs" ', and widen the field of knowledge. Probably too, like her father, she enjoyed danger and felt very ready to take risks in order to visit strange lands and peoples.

It does not follow that because Mary was to a quite unusual degree *unselfish* she was therefore *self-less*. There was a good deal of Kingsley toughness in her ego. Her books are full of herself—the self that was amused, the self that pursued knowledge under difficulties, and acquired irrepressible opinions. Both in speaking and writing she could be almost startlingly personal and direct, and her variegated style is all her own. But the often recurring pronoun 'I' in her books and lectures is not there because she wanted sympathy or admiration for herself; it is there because it was the best witness she had to the truth—

The First Journey

what she herself saw and experienced and thought, that was what she was sure of, and could speak of with confidence.

Her impulse to tell the unvarnished truth, and at the same time to present the suffering and pathos of the human scene through the veil of humour, gives to her writings an appearance of hardness. And hardness had indeed been bred in her. She had grown up on a diet of hard facts: the realities of her mother's illness and suffering, and her father's violent temper; and the contents of the books of travel and science in her father's library, in which there was little poetry or phantasy to be found. Her own mystical and pantheistic religion survived her agnostic upbringing, and she kept through life a habit of writing poetry, but the scientist in her overshadowed the poet. From early childhood her mind had been filled with histories of adventure crowded with scenes of brutality and cruelty. She set out for Africa inoculated, not in those days against the diseases which were the greatest danger, but against being shocked by almost any kind of barbarity. As we read her *Travels* we may sometimes feel shocked ourselves by the extent of her tolerance, unless we remember that it was a product of her environment, and moreover a most valuable part of her equipment as an explorer in West Africa.

Why did she choose West Africa—at that date a very dangerous part of the world? She herself suggests a number of reasons, some more convincing than others.

Soon after her parents' death she went for a trip to the Canaries—her first experience of travel and one which thrilled her. But she kept her eye on more things than the exquisite scenery of the Grand Canary. She noticed the excited and hilarious behaviour of homeward-bound traders who had, for the time, escaped the deadly fevers of 'The Coast'. She listened, though with slightly incredulous amusement, to the conversation of a trader invalided home, which 'consisted largely of anecdotes of friends of his, and nine times in ten he used to

Eight Years of Achievement

say, "He's dead now" '.[3] For most people this would have acted as a warning to keep away from the Coast, but Mary seems to have returned to England feeling that West Africa was where she wanted to go.

She declares that her main motive was a desire to finish an anthropological study of her father's. He had made notes on native customs and beliefs in many parts of the world, but had never been to Equatorial Africa. There were then few Europeans who had written about African ideas of religion and law, and information on these points, she said, was 'essential for my father's work. So I, knowing how much my father wished that book finished, went out after his death to West Africa, where all authorities agreed that Africans were at their wildest and worst. It was no desire to get killed and eaten that made me go and associate with the tribes with the worst reputation for cannibalism and human sacrifice, but just because such tribes were the best for me to study for what they meant by doing such things.' [4]

Quite apart from this aim of collecting the loose threads of her father's typical Kingsley dilettantism, there was that inclination of hers 'to associate with people who had something the matter with them'. There was plenty the matter with West Africans in the 1890's.

Perhaps the strongest motive was a personal one—to seek for the greatest possible contrast to long years of domestic imprisonment, and to be brought face to face with the spirit of nature at its wildest and most uncompromising. The 'Erdgeist', she says in her Memoir of her father, drew her as it did him more strongly than any other spirit; she wanted to spend at least a part of her life 'among non-human things'; and the way she fell in love with West Africa shows that she loved best the most inhuman and challenging aspects of nature. In a letter written after her two journeys she says, 'My people are mangrove swamps, rivers and the sea and so on. They never give

The First Journey

me the dazzles by their goings on like human beings do by theirs repeatedly.'[5]

One might have supposed that no human beings were so well calculated to give anyone the dazzles as those with whom she associated in Africa—the M'pongwes, and Igalwas, the Ajumbas and the Fans. But Mary found them much easier than English drawing-rooms, and this seems to have been partly because she felt sympathy, and even a certain kinship, with their outlook on life. She admits as much in her chapters on Fetish and in some passages of her letters.

As well as reasons she needed *excuses* for going alone to West Africa. Women only went there as wives of officials, or under the wing of missionary societies. Mary made zoology her excuse. On the suggestion of her Cambridge friend Dr Guillemard and of Dr Günther of the British Museum, she decided to 'collect specimens' of insects and fishes. Her sponsors did not expect much from this untrained amateur zoologist; moreover to collect and preserve fish is, according to Dr Günther, a laborious and rather expensive task, and Mary's means were slender. In the event she brought back some valuable specimens and some which were new to science (several hitherto unknown fish were called after her). Her success Dr Günther attributed to 'her extraordinary gift of observation', her 'judicious selection' and her 'indefatigable energy which overcame all obstacles'.

Definitely 'collecting' was a valid excuse. Less genuine was one she trumped up for the traders on her outgoing ship when they refused to believe that any sane person could go to the Coast for choice. She told them she was going to study the South Antarctic Drift. They thought this was a gold mine, but said they had never heard of it, and that anyway people who had anything to do with gold mines died even quicker than most.

For exploring the wildest regions she found trade the best excuse and the safest passport.

Eight Years of Achievement

Her material equipment caused her some trouble. Her friends expressed horror at her going at all, and when she remained determined, showered on her every kind of suitable and unsuitable medicament and comfort. Doctors reported that the Coast was 'the deadliest spot on earth' and advised frequent doses of quinine and the boiling of all drinking water. This advice Mary took. For first-hand information she was referred to the missionaries, many of whom seemed to have mysteriously survived on the Coast for a considerable time. 'So to missionary literature I addressed myself with great ardour; alas! only to find that these good people wrote their reports not to tell you how the country they resided in was, but how it was getting on towards being what it ought to be, and how necessary it was that their readers should subscribe more freely and not get any foolishness into their heads about obtaining an inadequate supply of souls for their money.' From the traders she did not at first seek information, as they were given such an appallingly bad name that they figured as among the worst dangers of the Coast.[6]

She tells us that she took a French word book of 'phrases in common use in Dahomey'. It appeared to contain the absurdities common to most foreign phrase books, with snippy examples of what the traveller would need to say. But it appeared that his needs would not be the usual ones. Mary gives some examples of these 'phrases in common use', running from 'Help, I am drowning' to 'Why has not this man been buried?' *Answer:* 'It is Fetish that has killed him and he must lie here exposed until only the bones remain.'[7]

In her personal kit she took an old pair of her brother's trousers—the only contribution he is ever reported to have made to her felicity—and owing to ineradicable Victorian modesty, a skirt to wear over the top of them. That skirt proved however to be useful as well as modest. In one of the wildest regions which she traversed on her second journey she

The First Journey

fell, she tells us, into a fifteen-foot deep game-trap, lined with spikes. 'It is at these times', she comments, 'that you realise the blessing of a good thick skirt. Had I paid heed to the advice of many people in England... and adopted masculine garments, I should have been spiked to the bone and done for. Whereas, save for a good many bruises, here I was with the fullness of my skirt tucked under me, sitting on nine ebony spikes some twelve inches long, in comparative comfort, howling lustily to be hauled out.' [8]

One valuable article for her equipment she had to do without. When on her second voyage she was planning to explore the Rapids of the Ogowé River in a native canoe she had some difficulty with the French authorities. They did not approve of her crew of Igalwas, and they said that the only other woman, a French lady, who had visited the Rapids had her husband with her. Mary replied that neither the Royal Geographical Society's list, in their *Hints to Travellers*, nor Messrs Silver in their elaborate lists of articles necessary for a traveller in tropical climates 'made mention of husbands'. Quite often she found she had to invent a husband to pacify the natives. It did not do when they asked 'Where is he?' to answer that she had not got one. 'I have tried it and it only leads to more appalling questions still.' She found that the best plan was to say that she was looking for him, and to 'locate him away in the direction in which you wish to travel; this elicits help and sympathy'.[9]

Finally she needed a ticket. She noted, with her usual grim humour, that the shipping agents did not issue return tickets on the West African lines of steamers.

She sailed from Liverpool in the beginning of August 1893.

Some years later she said of this departure into the unknown: 'Dead tired and feeling no one had need of me any more... I went down to West Africa to die. West Africa amused me

Eight Years of Achievement

and was kind to me and was scientifically interesting—and did not want to kill me just then. I am in no hurry. I don't care one way or the other for a year or so.' [10]

She began to be amused almost at once on sailing. By a wise instinct she had chosen, in spite of all she had heard said against traders, to go on a cargo boat. To that choice—to all that she learnt on that boat—she felt that she had owed her ability to survive in West African conditions. In the first chapter of *West African Studies* she writes: 'Doubtless a P. and O. is a good preparatory school for India, or a Union Castle for the Cape... but for the Bights, especially for the terrible Bight of Benin, "where for one that comes out there are forty stay in", I have no hesitation in recommending the West Coast cargo boat;... You must go on a steamer that has her saloon aft on your first trip out or you will never understand West Africa.'

The boat on which Mary made her first voyage had much the matter with it; so much that, with her usual tact, she refrains from mentioning its name, referring to it as 'the——'.*
The —— was dirty, over-loaded, yet so greedy for cargo that 'she shamelessly whistled and squarked for more' at every port. She was also 'wet', becoming 'nervous and femininely flurried when she saw a large wave coming'. When the saloon—which was duly aft—was threatened with a deluge, it was the practice to slam to the main door, stuff it with mats and yell 'Bill'. But during the first part of the voyage Bill never came; so Mary decided that the cry of 'Bill' was just an invocation to a weather god. Later however when the sea was still more threatening he did come and proved to be the steward. To the ——'s greed for cargo Mary seems to have owed the excellent notion of travelling among the natives as a trader. 'Everyone on board her she infected with a commercial spirit. I am not

* It appears from a letter of Mary's that the ship was called the *Lagos*.

The First Journey

by nature a commercial man myself, yet under her influence I found myself selling paraffin oil in cases in the Bights.'

The other passengers consisted of government officials and trading agents. They talked freely in Mary's presence of all the worst horrors of West Africa—fevers, parasites, insects, all forms of sudden death and hasty burial. They saw no reason to spare her, for either, they supposed, she was going to disembark at Canary, or she was one of the hated World's Women's Temperance Association whom it was desirable to frighten off at any price. But finding that she was firmly making for the Coast, that she was neither a missionary nor a Temperance Woman, they gradually accepted her as a friend, and passed on to her what useful hints they could.

The shy, severely dressed and apparently prim young woman surprised them all beyond measure. Not only did she know a great deal that they did not about the past history of the Coast in its days of slave-trading and piracy, but she knew quite a lot about its physical features—which parts of the coast were accessible, and which were suitable for trade. 'It was with a thrill of joy', she writes, 'that I looked on Freetown harbour for the first time in my life. I knew the place so well. Yes; there were all the bays, Kru, English and Pirate; and the mountains, whose thunder rumbling caused Pedro do Centra to call the place Sierra Leone when he discovered it in 1462. And had not my old friend, Charles Johnson, writing in 1724, given me all manner of information about it? . . . That those bays away now on my right were "safe and convenient for cleaning and watering", and so on; and there rose up before my eyes a vision of the society ashore here in 1724 that "lived very friendly with the natives—being thirty Englishmen in all; men who in some part of their lives had been either privateering, buccaneering, or pirating, and still retain the riots and humours common to that sort of life".' [11] Her familiarity with the riots and humours of that sort of life now stood her in good stead. For one thing

Eight Years of Achievement

there was the language matter. Once when she was small her father had overheard her indulging in some picturesque oaths. 'Where,' he angrily demanded of Mrs Kingsley, 'does this child get its language from?' 'Not from me,' Mrs Kingsley answered. The language used on a nineteenth-century cargo boat was probably far less rich than that to which Mary had become accustomed from her early reading, and having inherited her father's quick temper she understood the uses of bad language and appreciated its varieties. It was comfortable for the men on board the —— to notice that if their lady passenger inadvertently overheard something she should not, she remained unshattered. Every aspect of life on board fascinated and entertained her. She noted the peculiarities and prejudices of the crew, from first officer to cook, and watched, sometimes with a critical and rather mocking eye, the loading and unloading of cargo. From this she learned just exactly what kind and quantity of abuse it was proper and necessary to use towards African navvies and sailors, knowledge which was invaluable to her on her subsequent travels.

Her curiosity about all the details of navigation and her appreciation of its skills endeared her to the captain and crew. She became very friendly with Captain Murray, with whom she sailed again, though on a different boat, on her second voyage. She had already acquired, from hearing her father's talk about his own voyages and from reading, a considerable knowledge of seamanship. All this information she was soon to put into practice in Africa, learning to pilot small steamers across sandbars and up creeks, and becoming expert in managing a native canoe—a feat of which she was very proud.

Her practical ability, quick intelligence and intrepidity impressed the rough men she met on her travels, but rather naturally they felt unable to 'place' her. Who was she? and what was she really up to? After the publication of *Travels in West Africa* one old trader who had met her on Bonny River

The First Journey

wrote to another a letter which came into her hands, and which she quoted to George Macmillan. He had written that having seen her 'play bob-cherry with sharks on Lagos Bar' he had concluded she was just 'a holy terror'; but that when he had read her book he had to 'learn her over again' and make up his mind that she was a 'fine lady'. 'But how the ——, ——, ——, she got to know the truth about the Coast, he was ——d if he knew.' He knew that she had had a rare hard time of it on the Coast, and he had expected the Coast to catch it. It had, it appears, been a revelation to him that she had seen, understood, and forgiven so much.

What Mary on her side felt about the traders is revealed in many passages in her books. In *West African Studies* she writes:

'My first friends, among them my fellow-passengers on the ——, failing in inducing me to return from Sierra Leone did their best to save me by means of education. The things they thought I "really ought to know" would make wild reading if published *in extenso*. Led by the kindest most helpful of captains, they poured in information. . . . To my listening to everything that was told me by my first instructors, and believing it, undoubtedly I have often owed my life.'

And in *Travels in West Africa* she writes:

'One by one I took my old ideas derived from books and thoughts based on imperfect knowledge and weighed them against the life around me, and found them either worthless or wanting. The greatest recantation I had to make I made humbly before I had been three months on the Coast in 1893. It was of my idea of the traders. What I had expected to find them was a very different thing to what I did find them; and of their kindness to me I can never sufficiently speak, for on that voyage I was utterly out of touch with the governmental

Eight Years of Achievement

circles, and utterly dependent on the traders, and the most useful lesson of all the lessons I learnt on the West Coast in 1893 was that I could trust them. . . .

'Thanks to "the Agent", I have visited places I could never otherwise have seen; and to the respect and affection in which he is held by the native, I owe it that I have done so in safety. When I have arrived off his factory in a steamer or canoe, unexpected, unintroduced, or turned up equally unheralded out of the bush in a dilapidated state, he has always received me with that gracious hospitality, which must have given him under Coast conditions, very real trouble and inconvenience. . . . He has bestowed himself—Allah only knows where —on his small trading vessel so that I might have his one cabin. He has fished me out of sea and fresh water with boat-hooks; he has continually given me good advice and although he holds the meanest opinion of my intellect for going to such a place as West Africa for beetles, fish and fetish, he has given me the greatest assistance in my work.' [12]

Her ability to make friends with the traders, to sympathize with their hardships and appreciate their courage, not only helped her in her travels, it became one of the foundations of her subsequent political work. She came to believe that neither the missionaries nor the armchair idealists at home did half as much to civilize and promote good relations with the native Africans as did the traders on the spot, and those merchants, like John Holt of Liverpool, who had spent long periods on the Coast.

Some of her friendships with traders—with men often given to drunkenness and battered by intolerable conditions into the oddest eccentricities, endured for the rest of her life, as did many of her friendships with Africans. Her understanding of the hard life of the traders, and of the grim features of the country in which many of them had to work, can be illustrated

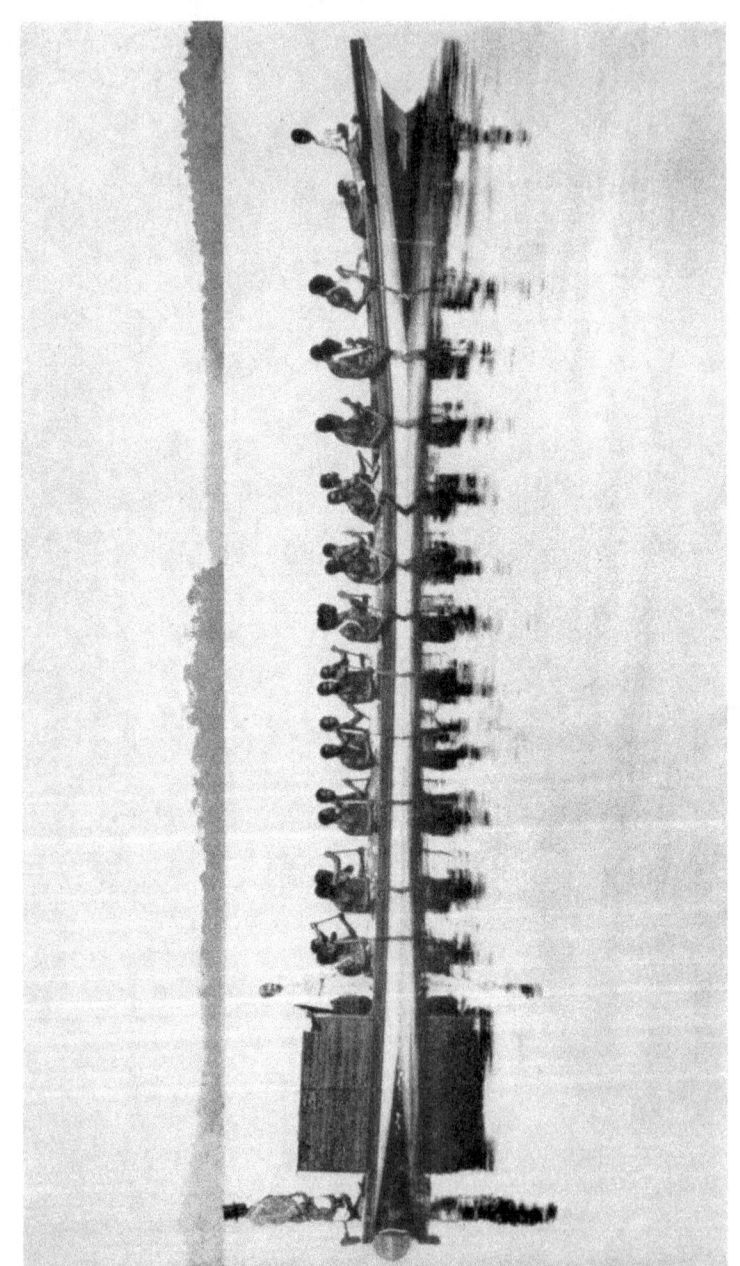

Trading canoe at Sette Cama, French Congo, 1899

The First Journey

by a fine passage in *West African Studies* describing the coast between Sierra Leone and Cape Palmas.

'Its appearance gives the voyager his first sample of those stupendous sweeps of monotonous landscape so characteristic of Africa. . . . A more horrible life than a life in such a region for a man who never takes to it, it is impossible to conceive; for a man who does take to it it is a sort of dream life. I am judging from the few men I have met who have been stationed here in the few isolated little factories that are established. Some of them look like haunted men. . . . The kind of country that produces this effect must be exceedingly simple in make: it is not the mere isolation from fellow white men that does it. This region of Africa from Sherboro to Cape Mount consists of four long lines—lines that go away into eternity as far as the eye can see. There is the band of yellow sand on which your little factory is built. This band is walled to landwards by a wall of dark forest, mounted against the sky to sea-ward by a wall of white surf; beyond that there is the horizon-bounded ocean. . . . In the light of brightest noon the forest wall stands dark against the dull blue sky, in the depth of the darkest night you can see it stand darker still against the stars; on moonlight nights and on tornado nights . . . it looks as if it had been done over with a coat of tar. The surf-wall is equally consistent, making the same sort of noise all the time. It is always white; in the sunlight, snowy white suffused with white mist wherein are little broken quivering bits of rainbows. In the moonlight it gleams with a whiteness there is in nothing else on earth . . . in the darkest of dark nights . . . it shows like a ghost of its daylight self, seeming to have in it a light of its own. . . . Night and day and season-changes pass over these things, like reflections in a mirror, without altering the mirror frame; but nothing comes that ever stills for one half second the thunder of the surf-wall, or makes it darker, or makes the

Eight Years of Achievement

forest-wall brighter than the rest of your world. Mind you, it is intensely beautiful, intensely soothing, intensely interesting if you can read it and you like it, but life for a man who cannot and does not is a living death.' [13]

One wonders if anyone had ever set so vividly before the minds of the British public the fate of some of those men who were making Britain rich.

Mary herself could read and could like this terrible land of West Africa. She fell under its spell with her eyes fully open to the merciless character of that grim Erdgeist.

On the run between Canary and Sierra Leone north-east trade winds at first blow cool and fresh—a coolness which is a danger to men returning home sick with fever, but a delight to the voyager outward bound. This fresh wind you lose as you close in to the coast by Cape Verde.

'It is the first meeting with the hot breath of the Bights that tries one; it is the breath of Death himself to many. You feel when you first meet it that you have done with all else; not alone is it hot, but it smells—smells like nothing else. It does not smell all it can then; by and by down in the Rivers, you get its perfection, but off Cape Verde you have to ask yourself, "Can I live in this or no?" and you have to leave it, like all other questions, to Allah, and go on.'

Before following her further as she went on let us listen to her own account of the spell which West Africa cast upon her. At the end of a lecture given to Cheltenham Ladies' College in 1898 she said:

'The charm of West Africa is a painful one. It gives you pleasure to fall under it when you are there, but when you get back here, it gives you pain, by calling you. It sends up before your eyes a vision of a wall of dancing, white, rainbow-gemmed surf playing on a shore of yellow sand before an audience of

The First Journey

stately cocoa-palms, or of a great mangrove-walled bronze river, or of a vast forest cathedral, and you hear, nearer to you than the voices of the people round you, nearer than the roar of the city traffic, the sound of that surf that is beating on the shore down there, and the sound of the wind talking in the hard palm leaves, and the thump of the natives' tom-toms, or the cry of the parrots passing over the mangrove swamps in the evening time—and everything that is round you grows poor and thin in the face of that vision, and you want to go back to the coast that is calling you, saying, as the African says to the departing soul of his dying friend, "Come back, this is your home." '

It was all very well of course, as Mary obviously felt, for a lonely eccentric like herself to risk her life for the magic of West Africa. She thought it her duty to warn others that this malarial, cannibal-haunted coast was not, as she might have said, everyone's cup of tea. She never minimized either the dangers or the acute discomforts which had to be faced; in fact she sometimes dwells upon the latter with an almost malicious relish. The conversation on board when it was not about death from fever was usually about insects; and Mary gained a good deal of information as well as some practical demonstrations. The —— carried with her a supply of large and over-friendly cockroaches; *en route* were added 'the flea line at Canary, mixed assortments at Sierra Leone, scorpions and centipedes in the Timber Ports, heavy cargo of the beetle and mangrove-fly line, with mosquitoes for dunnage, in the Oil Rivers'. But the insects ashore, Mary was warned, were much the worst, especially various species of ants. Yet insects were among the things she was out to collect; and during her first weeks on land she took she says, 'a general natural historical interest in them, with enthusiasm as of natural history; it soon became a mere sporting one, though equally

Eight Years of Achievement

enthusiastic at first'. She found that '75 per cent of West African insects sting, 5 per cent bite and the rest are permanently or temporarily parasitic on the human race'. She decided in the end that to 'keep quiet and not pay the least attention' was the best plan; and that anyway you had no chance in a stand-up fight with a West African insect. Nevertheless she did manage by her method of 'pursuing knowledge under difficulties' to collect interesting specimens; and she even learnt to eat insects in the form of the larvae of the big Rhinoceros Beetle. This was when she was in the wild forest regions known as the Bush, and here, to live at all, she had to eat what the Bushmen ate. She sets before her reader a detailed menu of what the British traders described with revulsion as 'native chop'. It included boa constrictor and crocodile, which last she found incurably 'musky' in flavour.

It is not easy to follow the course of her first voyage, for in her books she makes little distinction between the two. The first was mainly a preparation for the second and much longer journey which held most of her adventures and discoveries. But even on her short trip she covered an immense distance and acquired a great deal of useful knowledge, including some ability to make herself understood by the Africans.

They passed Cape Verde bound for Sierra Leone in late August, and the wet season was piling up its immense rain clouds and storms. It was here that Mary experienced her first tornado. Her books are written for the most part in an easy, digressive and informative style, but when she was moved to do so she could write pages of description as vivid as any in the English language.

'It was just south of Cape Verde that I met my first tornado. The weather had been wet in violent showers all the morning and afternoon. Our old Coasters took but little notice of it, resigning themselves to saturation without a struggle, pre-

The First Journey

vious experience having taught them it was the best thing to do, dryness being an unattainable state during the wet season, and "worrying one's self about anything one of the worst things you can do in West Africa". So they sat on deck calmly smoking, their new flannel suits, which were donned after leaving the trade winds, shrinking, and their colours running on to the deck, uncriticised even by the first officer. He was charging about shouting directions and generally making that afternoon such a wild, hurrying fuss about "getting in awnings", "tricing up all loose gear", such as deck chairs, and so on, to permanent parts of the ——, that, as nothing beyond showers had happened, and there was no wind, I began to feel most anxious about his mental state. But I soon saw that this activity was the working of a practical prophetic spirit in the man, and these alarms and excursions of his arose from a knowledge of what that low arch of black cloud coming off the land meant.

'We were surrounded by a wild, strange sky. Indeed there seemed to be two skies, one upper, and one lower; for parts of it were showing evidences of terrific activity, others of a sublime, utterly indifferent calm. At one part of our horizon were great columns of black cloud, expanding and coalescing at their capitals. These were mounted on a background of most exquisite pale green. Away to leeward was a gigantic black cloud-mountain, across whose vast face were bands and wreaths of delicate white and silver clouds, and from whose grim depths every few seconds flashed palpitating, fitful, vivid lightnings. Striding towards us across the sea came the tornado, lashing it into spray mist with the tremendous artillery of its rain, and shaking the air with its own thundergrowls. Away to windward leisurely boomed and grumbled a third thunderstorm, apparently not addressing the tornado but the cloud-mountain, while in between these phenomena wandered strange, wild winds, made out of lost souls frightened and

Eight Years of Achievement

wailing to be let back into Hell, or taken care of somehow by some one. This sort of thing naturally excited the sea, and all together excited the ——, who, not being built so much for the open and deep sea as for the shoal bars of West African rivers, made the most of it.

'In a few seconds the wind of the tornado struck us, screaming through the rigging, eager for awnings or any loose gear, but foiled of its prey by the first officer, who stood triumphantly on a heap of them, like a defiant hen guarding her chickens.' [14]

After the storms the rains came down in solid masses and for days nothing but steam and mist were visible. 'It was evening time when the —— reached that part of the South Atlantic Ocean where previous experience and dead reckoning led our Captain to believe that Sierra Leone existed.' It was necessary to remain for the night off shore, anchored and rolling. Many passengers were ill, but evidently not Mary. 'The mist, our world, went gently into grey, and then black, growing in a dense darkness filled with palpable, woolly, wet air, thicker far than it had been before. This, my instructors informed me, was caused by the admixture of "the solid malaria coming off the land".' When day came she was on deck to watch the dawn and was 'rewarded for my unwonted activity by a vision of beautiful earth-form dramatically unveiled. No longer was the —— our only material world. The mist lifted itself gently off, as it seemed, out of the ocean, and then separated before the morning breeze.' At night the masses of vapour returned and wrapped up the lovely harbour of Freetown for the night.

Although the beauty of Sierra Leone appealed to Mary, it was too sophisticated and luxurious for her liking; and she was not at all attracted by the westernized Africans whom she met there, flaunting their 'second-hand rubbishy white culture'. Later she was to contrast with the rudeness and self-importance

The First Journey

of these Sierra Leonians the dignity and courtesy which she found in other tribes—among them the cannibal Fans!

On leaving Sierra Leone they were immersed again in sopping vapour; everyone was wet, and everyone except Mary depressed. But the wet season 'did not operate in this manner on me; I had survived Sierra Leone, I had enjoyed it; why therefore not survive other places and enjoy them?' She had made up her mind, she says, never to oppose the spirit of the place whatever it might be, but rather 'to help it on'.

It was perhaps this heroic passivity—(what Mrs Green may have meant by 'profound obedience')—this desire to move with and understand rather than fight against the moods and manifestations of other forms of life which gave Mary her extraordinary immunity; her ability not only to resist disease, but to pass safely among wild beasts in the jungle and to win the confidence of the most dangerous native tribes, yet at the same time to control them for her own ends.

On the Grain Coast she had her first opportunity to learn something of one of the finest African tribes, the Kru, who worked in ships and ports. The Krumen had the distinction of having always refused to become slaves, or to traffic in slaves. But just as she had never expected to like traders, she had never, she says in an Appendix to her *Travels*, expected to like the Africans as a whole, but to find them degraded, savage and brutal. It was another 'error' she was destined to get rid of. Of the Kruboy she says: 'he is decidedly the most likeable of all Africans that I know.... In his better manifestations he reminds me of that charming personality, the Irish peasant.' But how to manage him was a lesson that needed learning. 'My first experience with him on a small Bush journey aged me very much,' she remarks.

At Calabar she met the Commissioner for the Oil Rivers, Sir Claude Macdonald, from whose kindness she was to profit on her second journey. From there she sailed down on the ——

Eight Years of Achievement

as far as St Paul de Loanda in Portuguese territory, where she stayed long enough to make some Portuguese friends and learn a little of the language. After that she went north again—presumably in coasting steamers, visiting on the way the Belgian Congo, the French Congo and the German territory of the Cameroons. Even these brief visits enabled her to gather much information about the methods of government in the different regions, and to form an opinion on their comparative merits.

She had studied the great period of Portuguese colonization in the fifteenth century, and was ironically amused at the primitive and ramshackle condition in which she now found the territory: officials lacking support and control from their home government; money sent out for roads, 'having a tendency—well, not to appear as roads'. But with typical impartiality she reveals that lamps for lighting Loanda sent from Britain turned out to be old gas lamps—and Loanda had no gas! (There seems to be a familiar ring about this story.)

She recognized at once how undesirable was the administration of the Belgian Congo; it was a part of the world, she said, where she would not travel again until it was in other hands. In the French Congo she spent a happy time, making a number of friends both French and English. She took every opportunity to get on good terms with any Africans she came across, but her technique was still unformed. It seems to have been during this visit to the French Congo that she had an adventure related in *West African Studies* under the heading 'Driver Ants'. It is an adventure which shows not only that Mary was not yet wise in regard to African behaviour, but also that she was still under the influence of the old days at home when she was always having to take responsibility for anything that was lost. She is describing the effect of a Driver Ant invasion on a native village.

'One minute there will be peace in the simple African home,

The First Journey

the heavy-scented hot night air broken only by the rhythmic snores and automatic side slaps of the family, accompanied outside by a chorus of cicadas and bull frogs. Enter the Driver— the next moment that night is thick with hurrying black forms, little and big, for the family, accompanied by rats, cockroaches, snakes, scorpions, centipedes, and huge spiders, animated by the one desire to get out of the visitors' way, fall helter-skelter into the street, where they are joined by the rest of the inhabitants of the village, for the ants when they once start on a village usually make a house-to-house visitation. I mixed myself up once in a delightful knock-about farce near Kabinda, and possibly made the biggest fool of myself I ever did. I was in a little village, and out of a hut came the owner and his family and all the household parasites pell mell, leaving the Drivers in possession; but the mother and father of the family, when they recovered from this unwonted burst of activity, showed such a lively concern, and such unmistakable signs of anguish at having left something behind them in the hut, that I thought it must be the baby. Although not a family man myself, the idea of that innocent infant perishing in such an appalling manner roused me to action, and I joined the frenzied group, crying "Where him live?" "In him far corner for floor!" shrieked the distracted parents, and into that hut I charged. Too true! There in the corner lay the poor little thing, a mere inert black mass, with hundreds of cruel Drivers already swarming upon it. To seize it and give it to the distracted mother was, as the reporter would say, "the work of an instant". She gave a cry of joy, and dropped it instantly into a water barrel, where her husband held it down with a hoe, chuckling contentedly. Shiver not, my friend, at the callousness of the Ethiopian; that there thing wasn't an infant—it was a ham!'

The whole subject of colonization, its history, objects and— where it had any—ideals, had long been of the greatest interest

Eight Years of Achievement

to Mary. It was obvious to her that the main reason for all such enterprises was to make money. But she saw also how much *amour propre* was involved in the possession of territories overseas, and in the French Congo, much though she liked it, she at first saw little else. It was a mystery, she felt, that France had persisted in her West African colonization, that 'she should have spent blood and money on it to the extent she has, does, and I am sure will continue to do, without its ever having paid her in the past, or paying her now, or being likely to pay her in the future. There are moments when it seems clear enough to me why she has done it but these moments only come when I am in an atmosphere reeking of La Gloire or La France—a thing I own I much enjoy; but when I am back in the cold intellectual greyness of commercial England, France's conduct in Africa certainly seems a little strange.' [15]

In the French Congo Mary made friends with a very unusual trader, Mr R. J. Dennett, a man who combined with the management of his factory a study of local tribes and conditions. He was an expert on the distribution of diseases such as sleeping sickness, and had already written a book about an African tribe, the Fjorts. To a second book, *The Folklore of the Fjorts*, Mary later contributed a preface.

From him she gained a lot of valuable information, and for him she felt a very real affection. Assuredly she did not pass along the coasts of West Africa like a non-human gust of wind. She brought to these lonely men living their strange lives isolated in the wilderness, warming and comforting gifts of sympathy and laughter.

Several years after her second journey was over, when she was longing and planning in vain to get back to the Coast, she wrote to Stephen Gwynn:

'I so often feel lonely away from men like Dennett and Parke and the rest of them; they are my people and their minds

The First Journey

are a print to me whether they are drunk or sober, sick or well, bad or good, or in their normal everyday state—mixed. . . . Dennett is, I grant, a bit more curious than the rest of us; the only thing in literature that is like him is Attwood in *The Ebb Tide* by Stevenson. . . . Did I ever tell you how when I was away with him at a very lonely hut-factory, where he was quite down on his uppers, he used to say in the evening as we sat in a murky little room illuminated by a wick floating in oil, burning faintly, then flaming, then going into a sort of fit and out with a fizzle, "Now let us have a little talk with God"? It was not praying, it was conversation with the Deity, respectful but familiar and now and then extremely critical, and I was never able to think it was queer of Dennett.'

From somewhere in the Cameroons—of whose efficient German government she approved—she sailed for home early in 1894.

She had learnt an immense amount; and one thing was that West Africa was 'not the restful kind of place I thought it, but just as fond of giving me odd jobs as up here has been'.*
Because she combined with the tolerance and love of adventure of the born traveller a spirit of true philanthropy and a constant feeling of responsibility, she had realized that there were two things which desperately needed to be done: one was to understand African culture and interpret it to the Colonial Office and the British public; the other to impress upon the authorities at home how much British traders were doing to propitiate and civilize the native tribes and increase the prestige and prosperity of Britain. Definitely, and for many reasons, she was going back.

'I succumbed to the charm of the Coast as soon as I left Sierra Leone on my first voyage out, and I saw more than enough during that voyage to make me recognise that there

* 'Up here' is used by Mary to mean the northern hemisphere.

Eight Years of Achievement

was any amount of work for me worth doing down there. So I warned the Coast I was coming back again and the Coast did not believe me; and on my return to it a second time displayed a genuine surprise, and formed an even higher opinion of my folly than it had formed on our first acquaintance, which is saying a good deal.'

3

The Second Journey: The Rivers

Our knowledge of Mary Kingsley's journeys has to be drawn almost entirely from her own accounts—from her books, lectures, and one or two letters written after her return. Few letters written during her travels seem to have survived. She kept very full diaries and her books are largely, she says, 'a sketchy résumé' of these. Stories of her own adventures have often to be extracted from chapters on African history and custom. She concludes the preface to her first book, *Travels in West Africa*, with these words:

'I have written only on things that I know from personal experience and very careful observation. I have never accepted an explanation of a native custom from one person alone, nor have I set down things as being prevalent customs from having seen a single instance. I have endeavoured to give you an honest account of the general state and manner of life in Lower Guinea and some description of the various types of country there. In reading this section you must make allowances for my love of this sort of country, with its great forests and rivers and its animistic-minded inhabitants, and for my ability to be more comfortable there than in England. Your superior culture-instincts may militate against your enjoying West Africa, but if you go there you will find things as I have said.'

When Mary set out for her second journey, on the steamer

Eight Years of Achievement

Batanga under her old friend Captain Murray, she was still comparatively unknown; but she had impressed some scientists at home and some administrators and traders on the Coast, and could look for more official support than she had had on her first solitary voyage. The kind of support which would involve supervision she did not want. It appears that she might have had financial grants to aid her in her anthropological and natural history researches but she refused them, travelling on her own small resources, augmented 'by doing a little in rubber and ivory'.[1] However, on this second voyage she had the status of travelling as what she calls 'honorary aide-de-camp' to Lady Macdonald, who was going out to join her husband, the Commissioner of the Oil Rivers. They sailed on 23 December 1894. When Lady Macdonald had, according to Mary, overcome her 'apprehension at the prospect of spending a month on board ship with a person so devoted to science as to go down the West Coast in its pursuit', the two women became fast friends. Mary was now herself in the proud position of an 'old Coaster' and was able to assist Lady Macdonald both on board and ashore. The Macdonalds on their side showed her great hospitality. Most of her time between January and May she spent either living with them or exploring in their neighbourhood.

During a visit with her hosts to the beautiful island of Fernando Po she made a study of its peculiar inhabitants, the Bubis, about whom very little had been written. She noted that they were strangely different from the natives on the mainland. Most Africans are inordinately fond of dress—in one form or another; but the Bubis seemed to dislike all clothes—with the exception of gaudy hats—and only to wear them when going shopping or working in the towns. She found among the Bubis 'a total lack of enthusiasm in trade matters, a thing which differentiates them more than any other characteristic from the mainlanders, who, young and old, men and women, regard

The Second Journey: The Rivers

trade as the great affair of life, take to it as soon as they can toddle, and don't even leave it off at death, according to their own accounts of the way the spirits of distinguished traders still dabble and interfere in market matters. But it is different with the Bubi. A little rum, a few beads, and finish.' [2]

Returning with the Macdonalds to Calabar, Mary devoted her time to 'puddling about the river and the forest' in search of fish and insects. During this period she went to visit Mary Slessor, the remarkable Presbyterian missionary who had lived for many years—for much of the time quite alone—in a settlement in the Calabar jungle.

Mary Kingsley was in general critical of missionaries, who nearly always, she thought, approached the natives in the wrong spirit and taught them the wrong things. But two of them, Mr Denis Kemp, head of the Wesleyan mission, whom she had met on the *Batanga*, and Mary Slessor, became her intimate friends.

She spent some time with Miss Slessor in the mission hut at Okyon, talking far into the tropical night of faith and fetish and the character of Africans. Though they differed very much in religious belief they were utterly at one in their feelings towards the Africans and their method of approaching them. This method which Mary Kingsley briefly describes as 'tact' had enabled Miss Slessor to win the trust and affection of the savage Okyon tribe, and to persuade them to abandon many of their most cruel practices and superstitions. Fundamentally this tact was in both women the product of a genuine respect for the African as a fellow creature—one who was also in his bewildered way seeking for the light. It derived in both of them from a profound humanity, and was accompanied, as indeed to succeed among the Africans it had to be, by indomitable courage. Like Mary Kingsley, Mary Slessor was extremely practical. She too believed in the civilizing influence of trade and had done much to encourage trading along the

Eight Years of Achievement

river from Okyon. Both women tempered their courage and seriousness with high spirits. There was a girlish gaiety and sense of fun in Mary Slessor which accorded well with her new friend's wealth of humour. The gaiety and the humour were passports to the hearts of Africans, who have a great love of laughter.

Before Mary sailed for home at the end of the year she paid Miss Slessor another visit—after that they did not meet again, though they frequently wrote to each other. Something of the admiration and love which Mary Kingsley felt for Miss Slessor is apparent from passages in her books and lectures. The deep impression she made on Miss Slessor in those two long visits we learn from letters written after Mary's death. In one to John Holt Miss Slessor wrote:

'I cannot yet realise that it is true that no more letters are to come, and that the long promised visit is never to be paid, and that that "something" which we were to attempt together is only to remain a dream. . . . Such friendships as Mary Kingsley's are not made often in one's life-time. The world is very much poorer to many as well as to me for her going, and the race in which we are most naturally interested and in that which concerns their welfare and development, will sadly miss and ever deplore the loss of her sympathetic heart and fertile brain. Richly gifted with a sense of humour, she could see all their follies and foolishness, but she never under-valued them as a race, and there was no sting or contempt in her joke or her laugh, and what is far more uncommon even with the missionaries, she respected their religious beliefs however foolish, and never either ridiculed or laughed at them.' [3]

Two years later Miss Slessor replied to a request for a fuller account of Mary Kingsley with a description which shows Mary's elusive personality in a fresh light. Reading it we are

Dug-out canoe, French Congo

Kabendas from South Congo

The Second Journey: The Rivers

reminded that, as Mary often said, she was more herself and more often happy when she was in West Africa.

'Oh dear me,' wrote Miss Slessor, 'to give you an account of Miss Kingsley and her stay here—you may as well tell me to catch the clouds with their ever-varying forms, or catch the perfume of our forest jessamine, or the flashes of the sunlight on the river. Miss Kingsley cannot be portrayed. She had an individuality as pronounced as it was unique, with charm of manner and conversation, while the interplay of wit and mild satire, of pure spontaneous mirth and of profoundly deep seriousness, made her a series of surprises, each one tenderer and more surprising than the foregoing. No! There was only one Miss Kingsley, and I can't define her character in the terms we speak of one another; or gather up the beauty and instruction and joy of those days of companionship—and say There! she gave me this or that other impression or impulse or idea.' [4]

The Calabar region, though it failed to give Mary as many rare fishes as she would have liked, provided her with great stretches of mangrove swamp to explore. There are in her pages many different accounts of these swamps into which she penetrated sometimes in company, often alone. She describes their fauna and flora, their intricate channels, the vast banks of stinking mud at low tide; their silences and weird noises, and the evidences of their gradual formation and their slow decay, as the soil held in the tall upstanding roots of the mangroves becomes solid enough for other trees, and the pines and palms and creepers grow down through the mangroves and dispossess them, leaving 'gaunt white skeletons standing on grey stuff that is not yet earth but is no longer slime'. At high tide it is possible to go among the trees for miles in a small canoe and this Mary did, having at least one narrow escape from a crocodile which got its forelegs over the end of her canoe.

Eight Years of Achievement

'I had to retire to the bows to keep the balance right, (it is no use saying because I was frightened, for this miserably understates the case) and fetch him a clip on the snout with a paddle, when he withdrew and I paddled into the very middle of the lagoon hoping the water was too deep there for him or any of his friends to repeat the performance.'

The creatures which inhabit the swamps are not of a vocal kind, so that the swamps are silent by day, at least during the dry season; 'in the wet season there is no silence night or day in West Africa but that roar of the descending deluge of the rain which is more monotonous and more gloomy than any silence can be.'

'But the mangrove swamp follows the general rule for West Africa, and night in it is noisier than the day. After dark it is full of noises; grunts from I know not what, splashes from jumping fish, the peculiar whirr of rushing crabs, and quaint creaking and groaning sounds from the trees; and—above all in eeriness—the strange whine and sighing cough of crocodiles. I shall never forget one moonlight night I spent in a mangrove swamp. I was not lost, we had gone away into the swamp from the main river, so that the natives of a village with an evil reputation should not come across us when they were out fishing. We got well in, on to a long pool or lagoon; and dozed off and woke, and saw the same scene around us twenty times in the night, which thereby grew into an aeon, until I dreamily felt that I had got into a world that was all like this, and always had been, and was always going to be so. Now and again the strong musky smell came that meant a crocodile close by, and one had to rouse up and see if all the crew's legs were on board, for Africans are reckless and regardless of their legs during sleep. On one examination I found the leg of one of my most precious men ostentatiously sticking out over the side of the canoe. I woke him with a paddle, and said a few words

The Second Journey: The Rivers

regarding the inadvisability of wearing his leg like this in our situation; and he agreed with me, saying he had lost a valued uncle, who had been taken out of a canoe in this same swamp by a crocodile. His uncle's ghost had become, he said, a sort of devil which had been a trial to the family ever since; and he thought it must have pulled his leg out in the way I complained of, in order to get him to join him by means of another crocodile. I thanked him for the information and said it quite explained the affair and I should do my best to prevent another member of the family from entering the state of devildom by aiming blows in the direction of any leg or arm I saw that uncle devil pulling out to place within reach of the crocodiles.' [5]

This passage is a perfect example of the playful and ironical humour which captivated Miss Slessor, and of that combination of 'tact' and authority which gave Mary her great influence over the Africans.

By the early spring she had determined to go further afield in search of 'fish and fetish'. All along the shores of West Africa the white man had left his traces, building towns and factories and separating the coastal tribes from their primitive roots and culture. The weaker tribes sought the protection of Europeans, and under that influence lost much of their own energy and simplicity—or so it seemed to Mary Kingsley. She wanted to see more of the unspoiled African and his native wilds. But as usual fish were her excuse. There were not enough rare fish in the Calabar region. The Niger would have seemed the obvious place for her to visit next, for while in England she had made the acquaintance of Sir George Goldie, the founder and head of the Royal Niger Company, whose wife later became her dearest friend, and Sir George was very ready to help her in her researches. She may have felt that he would have been too ready. He was a very determined man, and in the course of their long subsequent association they had many

Eight Years of Achievement

heated arguments. She came to have an immense admiration for his administration of the huge territories he had drawn together under the influence of the united traders who, through the granting of a royal charter, had become the Royal Niger Company. But this company was not popular with the rival administration of the Oil Rivers Protectorate, and Mary may have felt for this reason also that it would be more tactful not to pass immediately from the hospitality of Sir Claude Macdonald to that of Sir George Goldie. All she tells us is that she had 'private reasons' for not going to the Niger on this occasion.

She resolved to go instead to the Ogowé in the French Congo—'the greatest river between the Niger and the Congo', and one largely unexplored. This river runs far into the interior, and has hundreds of miles of dangerous rapids; along its banks lived, at any rate when Mary went there, 'notoriously savage tribes', chief among them the Fans.

Of this great region of wild country Mary writes in *West African Studies*: 'tribe after tribe come down into it, flourish awhile, and die, uninfluenced by Mohammedan or European culture. The Mohammedans in Africa have never mastered the western region of the forest belt; and the Europeans have never, in this region between Cameroon and Loango, established themselves in force. It is undoubtedly the wildest bit of West Africa.'[6]

It was therefore for her purposes of studying the natural African the most valuable. Of the Fans she says in the *Travels* that they are a great tribe 'that have in the memory of living men, made their appearance in the regions known to white men, in a state of migration seawards, and are a bright, active, energetic sort of African who by their pugnacious and predatory conduct do much to make one cease to regret and deplore the sloth and lethargy of the rest of the West Coast Tribes'.[7] The Fans were cannibals—and to some extent one

The Second Journey: The Rivers

gathers, still are, and addicted to human sacrifice. It was natural for Mary to want to go and 'find out what they meant by doing such things'. And the great African rivers and the mysteries of the dark forests held an infinite enchantment for her.

In order to get to Gaboon, whither she was first bound, she had to travel north to Lagos. This she did on her old friend the *Batanga*, then on a homeward voyage. She had to 'change' as she puts it, at Lagos Bar, 'which throws changing at Clapham Junction into the shade'. On the subject of Lagos Bar she is eloquent. 'Lagos is a marvellous manifestation of the perversity of man coupled with the perversity of nature, being at one and the same time one of the most important exporting ports on the West African seaboard, and one of the most difficult to get at.' *

Mary's crossing the bar on this occasion was one of the worst she had experienced. She had to pick up her southward bound steamer, the *Benguella*, on the far side of the bar, between which and the town of Lagos was a two-mile stretch of water, too shallow for most small coasters, wild with surf and infested with sharks. The *Benguella* was two days late, and the little branch boat tossed about in the broiling sun waiting for her. Finally Mary and another passenger took refuge in a larger steamer belonging to a German firm; and from there she was eventually safely conveyed to the *Benguella*. The other passenger was a very worried government official who had 'come out to see how a branch boat could get across the bar at low water'. He had found that it very nearly couldn't. He had been drenched and his boat awash, and he was in a great state of depression about Lagos Bar in general, and what could be done about it. Mary, who knew it better than he did, saw what was coming to him on this particular job. It is typical of

---

* It was more than twenty years after this date that the perversity of nature was finally overcome by the building of moles and the dredging of the channel.

Eight Years of Achievement

her that she took the trouble to find out later what did in fact come to him, and to inform her reader. 'He lived to earn the gratitude and esteem of Lagos and its government for his noble and determined services in working and surveying that awful bar. When, a few months after our amusing experiences on it, it went on worse than ever and vessel after vessel was wrecked, he rescued passengers and crews at great risk to his own life; for going alongside a vessel which is breaking up and in an open boat with a native crew, and getting off panic-stricken Africans and their belongings, surrounded by such a sea, with its crowd of expectant sharks, in the West African climate, is good work for a good man, and my fellow country-man did it, and did it well.' Mary loved to pay tribute to courage wherever she came across it.

She was now bent on travelling to a region where she would be out of reach of British counsellors and friends, her last contact being with a Mr Hudson, Agent-General of a big British company in the Ogowé region. She had met him on her first journey, and looked to him for help in getting up the river. She had also to propitiate the French authorities. One has the impression that to fulfil her ambitious projects she had to play off the one authority against the other, and that she managed to slip between the fingers of both.

She landed at Gaboon on 20 May 1895. Mr Hudson was away but other members of his firm—Messrs Hatton and Cookson—took charge of her, and saw her through the French Customs. Her account of these proceedings is taken from her diary.

'The officer is having his siesta but when aroused is courteous and kindly, but he incarcerates my revolver, giving me a feeling of iniquity for having had such a thing.' (Little did the gentleman know what sort of places this English lady was intending to visit.) 'I am informed if I pay 15/- for a licence

The Second Journey: The Rivers

I may have it—if I fire French ammunition out of it. This seems a heavy sum, so I ask M. Pichault, our mentor, what I may be allowed to shoot if I pay this? Will it make me free, as it were, of all local shooting? May I daily shoot governors, heads of departments, and *sous-officiers*? M. Pichault says "Decidedly not";—I may shoot "hippo or elephants or crocodiles". Now I have never tried shooting big game in Africa with a revolver, and as I don't intend to, I leave the thing in pawn. My collecting-cases and spirit, the things which I expected to reduce me to a financial wreck by customs dues, are passed entirely free, because they are for science. *Vive la France!*' [8]

Certainly Mary did not intend to shoot African animals, with a revolver or with anything else. The reason she gives for not doing this is characteristically unexpected. 'I am habitually kind to animals, and besides I do not think it is ladylike to go shooting things with a gun.' [9] So this very lady-like traveller pursued this particular adventurous journey unarmed (except, it later appears, for a bowie knife). By the natives in the coastal regions she was usually called 'Ma', but her wilder escorts in the bush addressed her as 'Sir'. She was not particular so long as she was obeyed.

There is no doubt that throughout her journeys Mary was playing with death—she may indeed have been courting it, as the passage quoted about her first departure rather implies. She certainly took pleasure in the game. She found fascination and peace in a communion with nature where the motive of self-preservation was in abeyance, and the individual was thrown back on a solitary self-dependence without limit.

She played with death in many forms; among wild beasts in swamp and jungle; on the rapids of the Ogowé; alone among fierce tribes of whom even other kindred tribes were desperately afraid; and constantly wherever she went with death

Eight Years of Achievement

in the shape of fever. This, the most prevalent danger, she seems not to have feared at all. Fever lurked in the mists—and she loved the mists, as they streamed out to sea from the coasts, or rose up from the mangrove swamps.

'The mist comes stretching out from under the bushes over the sand towards the sea, now raising itself up into peaks, now crouching down upon the sand, and sending out long white arms of feelers towards the surf and then drawing them back as if it were some spirit-possessed thing, poisonous and malignant, that wanted to reach us, and yet is timorous and frightened of the surf's thunder-roar and spray. It gets over its alarm after about an hour, however, and comes curling out in a white wall and during the rest of the calm before the dawn-wind comes, wraps itself round us, dankly smelling like some foul corpse.

'I don't think this sort of mist is healthy, but it is often supremely lovely and always fascinates me. I have seen it play the weirdest wildest tricks many times, in many a place in West Africa. I have when benighted walked hurriedly through it for miles in the forest while it has mischievously hidden the path at my feet from the helpful illumination of the moon, swishing and swirling round my moving skirts. I have seen it come out of the forests and gather on the creek before and round me when out o' nights in canoes, gradually as we glided towards the breeze-swept river, forming itself into a great ball which has rolled before us, showing dimly now in the shadow, ghostly white now in the moonshine, and bursting into thousands of flakes if the river breeze when it met it was too strong for it; if it were not, just melting away into the sheet of mist that lay sleeping on the broad river itself. Now and again you will see it in the forest stretch up a gradually lengthening arm, and wind it lazily round and round some grand column of a tree stem, to the height of ten or twenty

The Second Journey: The Rivers

feet from the ground, spread out its top like a plume and then fall back again to the mist river from which it came. . . . I have often, when no one has been near to form opinions of my frivolity, played with it, scooping it up in my hands and letting it fall again, or swished it about with a branch, when it lay at a decent level of three or four feet from the ground. When it comes higher and utterly be-fogs you, you don't feel much inclination to play with it.' [10]

During the ten days she spent at Gaboon Mary did some collecting and made her first acquaintance with the Fans. The Fans of this district were very mild examples, but even they were regarded with fear and suspicion. On several occasions she met one on a lonely walk, and recollecting advice given her by 'old Captain Boler of Bonny'—'Be afraid of an African if you can't help it, but never show it anyhow', entered into conversation—in what language she does not tell us; probably it was in trade English—she later learned a good deal of the Fans' own language. Meeting a Fan hunter on one occasion on a lonely path she introduced herself with a gift of tobacco, discussed sport, and 'on parting I gave him some more tobacco, because he kindly gave me a charm to enable me to see things in the forest. He was gratified, and said "you ver nice", "Goodbye", "Good day", "So long", "Good night", which was very nice of him, as these phrases were evidently all the amiable greetings in English that he knew. The "so long" you often hear the natives in Gaboon say; it always sounds exceedingly quaint. They have of course picked it up from the American missionaries, who have been here upward of thirty years.'

A little river trade steamer, the *Mové*, took her from Gaboon up the Ogowé as far as Lambarene—now made famous by Dr Schweitzer's hospital. The voyage lasted several days, and the views on the river impressed Mary deeply. The forest along the banks she found 'beyond all my expectations of tropical

Eight Years of Achievement

luxuriance and beauty, and it is a thing of another world to the forest of the upper Calabar, which beautiful as it is is a sad dowdy to this. . . . The climbing plants are finer than I have ever before seen them. They form great veils and curtains between and over the trees, often hanging in stretches of 30 to 40 ft or so wide and 30 to 60 or 70 feet high. Sometimes these curtains are decorated with large bell-shaped bright coloured flowers, sometimes with delicate sprays of white blossoms . . . every now and then a soft sweet heavy breath of fragrance comes out to us as we pass by.'

Although Mary was later to criticize the part played by many African Missions in the education of natives, she owed much during her travels to the kindness of individual missionaries; and not least, though she does not specifically mention it, that through them she was provided with one or two Christians among her native crews who knew some English as well as a few European rules of conduct. At Kangwe near Lambarene she stayed in the house of M. and Mme Jacot. Her diary of this stay is, she says, 'a catalogue of the collection of fish . . . and a record of the continuous never-failing kindness and help that I received from M. and Mme Jacot, and of my attempts to learn from them the peculiarities of the region, the natives, and their language and customs, which they both knew so well and manage so admirably. I daily saw there what it is possible to do, even in the wildest and most remote regions of Africa, and recognised that there is still one heroic form of human being whose praise has never adequately been sung, the missionary's wife.'

What she describes as her first visit to 'a Fan fireside' occurred at this time. She was wandering through the bush doing her best to avoid the Fans, being 'nervous of them from information received', but she took a wrong path and ended by falling through the roof of a Fan hut concealed in a hollow among undergrowth. 'What the unfortunate inhabitants were doing,

The Second Journey: The Rivers

I don't know, but I am pretty sure they were not expecting me to drop in, and a scene of great confusion occurred. My knowledge of Fan dialect then consisted of "Kor Kor", so I said that in as fascinating a tone as I could, and explained the rest with three pocket handkerchiefs, a head of tobacco and a knife, which providentially I had stowed away in what my nautical friends would call my after-hold—my pockets . . . I squared the family all right.'

One sometimes wonders what Mary's after-hold can have looked like; for she was always able to produce from it some propitiatory article of the kind she mentions; and on this ability her life occasionally depended.

From Lambarene she went on ninety miles up river to Njolé, the last port for the river steamers, and the end of things European for five hundred miles; after that all traffic had to be by canoe as nothing else could pass up the hundreds of miles of rapids.

A French official at Njolé conveyed to her—in the language of ejaculation and signs, for she knew almost no French—how formidable these rapids were. Her reactions were what one has learnt to expect. 'Wish to goodness I knew French, for wishing to see these rapids, I cannot help feeling anxious and worried at not fully understanding this dramatic entertainment regarding them.' She returned down river as far as Talagouga, a little above Lambarene, and stayed once more with hospitable missionaries, M. and Mme Forget and M. and Mme Gaçon. She set to work on her plan to visit the rapids, once again, one suspects, using fish-collecting as an excuse—for how could she expect to catch fish, let alone bring them back in bottles from among those wild waters? Meantime she engaged in a kind of trade with the Fans, buying specimens of fish from them. They 'wanted enormous prices . . . but I confess I rather enjoy the give-and-take fun of bartering . . . and my trading with them introduced us to each other so that when we met in the

Eight Years of Achievement

course of the long climbing walks I used to take beetle-hunting in the bush behind the mission station, we knew about each other and did not get much shocked or frightened. . . . That forest round Talagouga was one of the most difficult bits of country to get about in I ever came across, for it was dense and there were no bush paths. No Fan village wants to walk to another Fan village for social civilities, and all their trade goes up and down the river in canoes.' 'Talagouga is grand, but its scenery is undoubtedly grim, and its name signifying the gateway of misery, seems applicable. It must be a melancholy place to live in, the very air lies heavy and silent. I never saw the trees stirred by a breeze the whole time I was there. The only sign of motion you get is in the Ogowé; if you look at it you see, in spite of its dark quiet face, that it is sweeping past at a terrific pace. Every now and then you will notice a canoe full of wild, naked, or nearly naked savages, silent because they are Fans, and don't sing like Igalwas or M'pongwe in canoes.' The occasional uncanny silence of these savages, and the unearthly silence of the forests till they were suddenly rent by tornadoes, were terrors with which Mary was to become still better acquainted. Pushing through the dense curtains of creeper in the Talagouga jungle among fallen timber infested with red driver ants, scorpions and snakes of all shapes and shades, she pursued her researches, bottling occasional rare snakes which she caught in cleft sticks. 'Several times when further in the forest, I came across a trail of flattened undergrowth, for 50 or 60 yards, with a horrid musky smell that demonstrated it had been the path of a boa constrictor.'

The voyage up the rapids was no easy thing to arrange.[11] 'No one whom I could get hold of regarded it as feasible.' But she steadily increased the bribe she offered in food and wages to a native crew, and finally M. Gaçon agreed to lend her a canoe and two English-speaking Igalwas who had been part of the way up the river before. It was proposed to complete the crew

The Second Journey: The Rivers

with six local Fans. But 'the Fans round Talagouga wouldn't go at any price above Njolé, because they were certain they would be killed and eaten by the up-river Fans'. Finally more Igalwas and some M'pongwe—both reputable tribes—were borrowed from Hatton and Cookson's factory near by, and after a farewell from her French friends which suggested they did not expect to see her again, Mary set off. Mme Forget had lent her, she says, three hairpins. There was a constant drain on her hairpins in Africa—they are the sort of thing easily lost in rapids or dark forests, and Mary was always trying to renew her stock. She found them useful not only for fastening up her hair. 'Remember', she remarks in *Travels in West Africa*, 'that whenever you see a man, black or white, filled with a nameless longing, it is tobacco he requires. Grim despair accompanied by a gusty temper indicates something wrong with his pipe, in which case offer him a straightened-out hairpin.'

The canoe set off with Mary ensconced at the stern, her portmanteau and her invaluable trade box at her back, and the French flag on a stick floating behind her. She was not yet an expert canoeist, and the control of navigation was entrusted to a head man named M'bo. Fresh trouble occurred at Njolé, as the French authorities disapproved of the whole excursion on the ground that there was the wrong kind of crew, and the lady passenger had not got a husband with her, but they were talked round and agreed to wash their hands of all responsibility.

The boatload was a merry one, and with much splashing, singing and shouting the canoe was forced up against the swift current. There were frequent occasions when it had to be dragged by hand round a rocky point surrounded by whirlpools and Mary was then ordered by M'bo to 'jump for bank, sah.' Altogether it was anything but a silent journey. The roar of the water steadily increased. At the Fan villages where they had spent their first few nights there was much shouting, arguing and barking of dogs on their arrival. Whenever the

Eight Years of Achievement

going was smooth enough for a little relaxation the crew sang M'pongwe songs, and Mary gives an amusing and instructive description of these, showing the passionate interest most Africans take in trade and the acquisition of a little property—especially clothes.

'My crew sing M'pongwe songs, descriptive of how they go to their homes to see their wives, and families and friends, giving chaffing descriptions of their friends' characteristics and of their failings, which cause bursts of laughter from those among us who recognise the allusions; and how they go to their boxes, and take out their clothes and put them on—a long bragging inventory of these things is given by each man as a solo, and then the chorus, taken heartily up by his companions, signifies their admiration and astonishment at his wealth and importance—and then they sing how, being dissatisfied with that last dollar's worth of goods they got from "Holty's", they have decided to take their next trade to Hatton and Cookson, or *vice versa*; and then comes the chorus, applauding the wisdom of such a decision, and extolling the excellence of Hatton and Cookson's goods or Holty's. The words are put in by the singer on the spur of the moment, and only restricted in this sense that there would always be the domestic catalogue ... sung to the one fixed tune, the trade information sung to another, and so on.'

The first few villages where they could stay overnight had been recommended because two Frenchmen exploring the Ogowé had stayed there safely two years before. All went well till a night came when the canoe was overturned among rocky reefs at nightfall, out of sight of any village. One was eventually discovered; but its inhabitants, painted vermilion all over, were busy dancing round a fire. Luckily curiosity ensured a reasonable reception for the strangers, and Mary was given a queer semi-ruined hut for her headquarters; there she sat to guard

The Second Journey: The Rivers

her boxes, surrounded by staring natives. Two among these, the chiefs of the village, 'had on old French military coats in rags; but they were quite satisfied with their appearance, and evidently felt through them in touch with European culture, for they lectured to the others on the habits and customs of the white man with great self-confidence and superiority'.

Some of these natives informed Mary that the Ogowé rapids were at their worst just then, and that a young French official had been drowned there the year before.

Late that night, leaving the hut in the charge of some of her crew, Mary went off alone to have yet another look at this fascinating and deadly river.

'The moon was rising, illuminating the sky, but not yet sending down her light on the foaming, flying Ogowé, in its deep ravine. The scene was divinely lovely; on every side out of the formless gloom rose the peaks of the Sierra del Cristal. . . . In the darkness round me flitted thousands of fireflies, and out beyond this pool of utter night flew by unceasingly the white foam of the rapids; sound there was none save their thunder. The majesty and beauty of the scene fascinated me, and I stood leaning with my back against a rock pinnacle watching it. Do not imagine it gave rise, in what I am pleased to call my mind, to those complicated, poetical reflections natural beauty seems to bring out in other people's minds. It never works that way with me; I just lose all sense of human individuality, all memory of human life, with its grief and worry and doubt, and become part of the atmosphere. If I have a heaven, that will be mine, and I verily believe that if I were left alone long enough with such a scene as this or on the deck of an African liner in the Bights, watching her funnel and masts swinging to and fro in the great long leisurely roll against the sky, I should be found soulless and dead; but I never have a chance of that.'

She had no chance that night, for her foretaste of Nirvana was

Eight Years of Achievement

presently shattered by a terrific yell. Hurrying in the direction of the shriek, expecting murder, she found that one of her crew had gone to sleep beside a slowly burning log of their bonfire, and the fire had crept along under him. 'The shriek was his way of mentioning the fact.'

As the canoe struggled up-stream signs of human habitation became rare, the banks wilder and more mountainous, and the raging river more full of dangerous rocks and whirlpools. After a while a new and still more ominous sound could be heard above the roar of the Ogowé. 'I said to M'bo: "That's a thunderstorm away among the mountains." "No sir," says he, "that's the Alemba." '

The falls of the Alemba when Mary got close to them filled her with awe—they were unlike anything she had ever before seen or heard. 'Those other rapids are not to be compared to it; they are wild, headstrong and malignant enough, but the Alemba is not as they. It does not struggle, and writhe, and brawl among the rocks, but comes in a majestic springing dance, a stretch of waltzing foam, triumphant.'

When they finally turned for home there were still worse dangers to encounter, for it is harder to steer a canoe going with the current than one beating up against it. Whenever the canoe got wedged among rocks everyone had to get out of it, either on to the rocks or into the water. Once when this happened at night only seven of the party could be collected again and Mary feared that one of the crew was drowned. But at last above the clamour of the rapids an agonized voice was heard howling out 'the strains of that fine hymn *Notre Port est au Ciel*—which is a great favourite hereabouts owing to its noble tune. We picked the singer off his rock, and then dashed downwards to further dilemmas and disasters.'

Safely back in Lambarene, Mary set about teaching herself, at considerable risk, how to manage a small canoe singlehanded.

The Second Journey: The Rivers

Her further adventures and explorations were mainly on the north bank of the lower Ogowé, the Orungo region, a wild and little-known district inhabited by what she describes as 'unadulterated Africans'—mostly cannibal Fans. Chapter XI of *Travels in West Africa* gives some account of the most important of her explorations in this region, but many of her adventures found no place in her books—partly because she was afraid of not being believed. Fortunately she related some of them in lectures and letters. The heading of Chapter XI is characteristic: 'In which the voyager goes for bush again and wanders into a new lake and a new river.'

4

The Second Journey: 'Going for Bush'

'On first entering the great grim twilight regions of the forest you hardly see anything but the vast column-like grey tree stems in their countless thousands around you, and the sparsely vegetated ground beneath. But day by day, as you get trained to your surroundings, you see more and more, and a whole world grows up out of the gloom before your eyes. Snakes, beetles, bats and beasts, people the region that at first seemed lifeless.

'It is the same with the better lit regions, where vegetation is many-formed and luxuriant. As you get used to it, what seemed at first to be an inextricable tangle ceases to be so . . . daily you find it easier to make your way through what looked at first an impenetrable wall. . . .

'There is the same difference also between night and day in the forest. You may have got fairly used to it by day, and then some catastrophe keeps you out in it all night, and again you see another world. To my taste there is nothing so fascinating as spending a night out in an African forest . . . but, I do not advise anyone to follow the practice. Nor indeed do I recommend African forest life to anyone. Unless you are interested in it and fall under its charm, it is the most awful life in death imaginable. It is like being shut up in a library whose books you cannot read, all the while tormented, terrified, and bored. . . . Still it is good for a man to have experience of it, whether

The Second Journey: 'Going for Bush'

he likes it or not, for it teaches you how very dependent you have been during your previous life on the familiarity of those conditions you have been brought up among, and on your fellow-citizens; moreover it takes the conceit out of you pretty thoroughly during the days you spend stupidly stumbling about among your new surroundings.

'When this first period passes there comes a sense of growing power. The proudest day in my life was the day on which an old Fan hunter said to me—"Ah! you *see!*" Now he did not say this, I may remark, as a tribute to the hard work I had been doing in order to see, but regarded it as the consequence of a chief having given me a little ivory half-moon, whose special mission was "to make man see Bush", and when you have attained to that power in full, a state I do not pretend to have yet attained to, you can say, "put me where you like in an African forest, and as far as the forest goes, starve me or kill me if you can".

'As it is with the forest, so it is with the minds of the natives. Unless you live alone among the natives, you never get to know them; if you do you gradually get a light into the true state of their mind-forest. At first you see nothing but a confused stupidity and crime; but when you get to see—well! as in the other forest,—you see things well worth seeing.'[1]

To see more, both of the forest and the mind-forest, was Mary's constant aim, and to do this she had now to make far more dangerous excursions than any she had yet made. She planned to go alone with whatever native crew she could collect, into regions where no white person had ever been before. For self-protection she was to rely on the disarming character of trade. She often refers in her books to this 'reasonable' method of approach, but never stated her ideas on the subject so fully as in the lecture she gave to Cheltenham Ladies' College.

'I find I get on best by going among the unadulterated

Eight Years of Achievement

African in the guise of a trader; there is something reasonable about trade to all men, and, you see, the advantage of it is that, when you first appear among people who have never seen anything like you before, they naturally regard you as a devil; but when you want to buy or sell with them, they recognize that there is something human and reasonable about you. . . .

'The trading method enables you to sit as an honoured guest at far-away inland village fires; it enables you to become the confidential friend of that ever-powerful factor in all human societies, the old ladies. It enables you to become an associate of the confraternity of Witch Doctors, things that being surrounded with an expedition of armed men must prevent your doing.' (She does not add here that she was also able to become expert in native criminal law, and a judge and peace-maker in some very dangerous quarrels.) She goes on: 'The worst of the trading method is it entails on you an unfashionable degree of hard work on your elementary subjects—namely the details of the West Coast trade.'

She was not the first to use trade as a means to anthropological study, and in another lecture she referred to Habbe Scheiden who had travelled as a trader. But, she added, 'he was not a success as a trader. That so-called "simple child of Nature" the African, swindled that distinguished scientific man in his trade sadly. But he got what he wanted, a wonderful knowledge of the native mind and ideas, and I followed humbly in his footsteps, avoiding being swindled as much as possible by giving great attention to trade matters before I went in for them.' One would not expect a Kingsley to submit to being swindled, and a delightful postscript to this passage is to be found in a letter to John Holt, written on 14 November 1898. One of her problems as an honest trader was to avoid undercutting other traders. 'I was let out into the bush', she explains to Mr Holt, 'with horrid threats as to what would happen to

The Second Journey: 'Going for Bush'

me if I spoilt prices; I was brought up to ask three times as much as I ever expected to get and seven times as much as I deserved. I remember coming into one of H. and C's factories with 30 lbs. of rubber. "What did you pay for that?" said the agent. I told him, and to this day I remember the tone of voice with which he said as he rose from his chair, "Miss Kingsley, that I should ever live to see this day! You've been swindling those poor blacks!" We had a simply awful row.' [2]

One trading expedition of hers must have taken place soon after her visit to the rapids, and will have been intended to give her a little more practice in associating with the Fans before embarking on her more ambitious expedition to the Rembwé. She makes no mention of this excursion in her books, but related it in her Cheltenham lecture. She describes it as a first experience of trading—but she presumably means of solitary trading—and as one 'ignorantly embarked on in the middle of the terrible Ba-Fan tribe, and in a region made in a wild way, adjoining the Sierra del Cristal range, where it meets the Ogowé upper basin in the Okono affluent'.

'I had made friends with three choice spirits, ivory traders of the Ajumba tribe, and I persuaded them to let me go with them on one of their trips after ivory. They were to take me and my little belongings in their canoe to a village, and were to give me a most excellent character to the local nobility and gentry. I told them what to say, and paid them for saying it, to prevent mistakes, and then they were to leave me there and go higher up the river on their own business, and call for me on their way down. They duly took me, gave the village the idea that I was *just* the sort of thing to improve the local social tone, and left me. I was horribly nervous when they did, for on our way up to it we had come across a gentleman who danced and howled on the bank, and wanted to sell something badly as we were a trading company. We went for him like an arrow,

Eight Years of Achievement

thinking it might be a tooth—an elephant's I mean, not his own. It wasn't—it was a leg—not his own either, but the leg of a gentleman of some kind. This upset my companions and made them sick, and it and their conversation on those Fans which followed, made me nervous.'

During her first night alone in this village a frenzied hippopotamus which had become separated from the herd tore at full tilt through the village street, crashing into houses, and causing panic and rage among the inhabitants. By the time this crisis was over, it was morning; Mary never seems to have got much sleep on her expeditions.

'The next morning the Fans turned their attention to me, and started selling to me their store of elephant tusks and india rubber. . . . I did not want those things then, but still felt too nervous of the Fans to point this out firmly, and so had to buy. I made it as long an affair as I could . . . and I gradually found myself the proud owner of balls of rubber and a tooth or so and alas! my little stock of cloth and tobacco all going fast. Now, to be short of money anywhere is bad, but to be short of money in a Fan village is extremely bad, because these Fans, when a trader has no more goods to sell them, are liable to start trade all over again by killing him, and taking back their ivory and rubber and keeping it until another trader comes along. . . . So I kept my eye up-river most anxiously on the look-out for my black trader friends' canoe, and for days in vain. All my trader stuff was by now exhausted, and I had to start selling my own belongings, and for the first time in my life I felt the want of a big outfit. My own clothes I certainly did insist on having more for, pointing out that they were rare and curious. A dozen white ladies' blouses sold well. I cannot say they looked well when worn by a brawny warrior in conjunction with *nothing* else but red paint and a bunch of leopard tails, particularly when the warrior failed to tie the strings at

The Second Journey: 'Going for Bush'

the back. But I did not hint at this, and I quite realise that a pair of stockings can be made to go further than we make them by using one at a time and putting the top part over the head and letting the rest of the garment float on the breeze. But I had too few, and they were all gone before that canoe came, indeed everything but what I stood up in was. The last thing I parted with was my tooth-brush, and the afternoon *that* had gone, down came the canoe, just as I was making up my mind to set up in business as a witch-doctor. The black traders said they were very glad to see me again, but I should have a very hard time if I came down with them, because *they* had sold right out, and therefore dared not call at any village before reaching the main river. I said, "Oh, don't mention that, *pray*. I'll come with you", and so to the grief of those Fans I left them.'

The reader will have noticed that Mary admits to being frightened on many occasions. The idea that she simply did not feel fear gained currency from a letter published after her death in the *Spectator*. The writer said he had asked her if she felt fear, and she had said she did not, for if she once did she felt she would collapse entirely. All she felt in the face of instant danger was 'a strong salt taste in my mouth. Whenever I feel *that*, I know I've got to take myself as seriously as I know how.' She had obviously the kind of presence of mind which excludes every other sensation—for the moment. She explains her reactions more clearly in a passage of *West African Studies* relating some encounters with wild beasts.

'My nervousness regarding the big game of Africa is of a rather peculiar kind. I can confidently say that I am not afraid of any wild animal—until I see it—and then—well I will yield to nobody in terror; fortunately my terror is a special variety; fortunately because no one can manage their own terror. . . . You can suppress alarm, excitement, fear, fright, and all those small-fry emotions, but the real terror is as dependent on the

Eight Years of Achievement

inner make of you as the colour of your eyes, or the shape of your nose; and when terror ascends its throne in my mind I become preternaturally artful, and intelligent to an extent utterly foreign to my true nature.' ³

On 22 July 1895 Mary entered in her diary 'Left Kangwe'. It was a truant expedition, for this time she did not fly the French flag, and had no governmental or Trade House protection. M. Jacot had befriended her by finding her four Ajumbas for crew, two of whom were Christians. She had also an Igalwa named N'gouta for interpreter. She started out with a severe headache and the conviction she was in for a bout of fever, but as she found a native canoe one of the most comfortable places to be in she saw no reason for delay. Every canoe they passed shouted a greeting and asked where they were going. 'We say "Rembwé"—and they say "*What!* Rembwé!"—and we say "Yes, Rembwé", and paddle on.' The answer naturally caused surprise. The Rembwé (on French maps Ramboué) is a river running into the Gaboon estuary. It runs northwards, and rises among the mountains of the Ouronogou district on the north side of the watershed which feeds the Ogowé. It is therefore not connected with any branch of the Ogowé, yet it was up one of these branches that Mary was going in quest of it.⁴ The maps available at that time were very inadequate, and she soon entered uncharted country. She had to travel largely by hearsay, and hearsay could be confusing. 'These good people', she says, 'call a river by one name when you are going up it, and by another when you are going down.' Different tribes called the same place by different names; and Europeans attempting to make maps had 'solemnly set down' various forms of the native words for 'I don't know' as the names of villages and rivers.* But her sense of the geographical lie of country

---

* In a letter to the *Spectator* in December 1895 Mary, while defending the character of the Africans she had known, admitted their lack of technical ability, and she wrote: 'I am personally acquainted to the point

The Second Journey: 'Going for Bush'

was singularly acute, and she knew quite well that she would have to go part of the way overland—leaving behind what little civilizing influence the waterways, even the most remote, had on the local tribes.

She began by not liking any of her crew; she never liked them as well as the Fans she picked up *en route*. On the second day she agreed to take on a man who was wanting to get work in John Holt's factory on the Rembwé, and was at a loss how to get there. A few days later an uninvited Fan also joined them—without pay, and purely, Mary thought, to see the fun and pick up the pieces after any fights. This gentleman had the 'manners of a duke and the habits of a dust-bin'. At any halt he would sit next her and appropriate the tobacco tin. When he had filled his pipe, courtesies would pass between them which she renders as follows: ' "My dear Princess, could you favour me with a lucifer?" I used to say "My dear Duke, charmed, I'm sure", and give him one ready lit.' The duke, as she always calls him, wore nothing but a small dirty loin-cloth, but he carried a magnificent gun.

They spent their first night at a very respectable Ajumba village where one of the crew had a house, and where a man from Kangwe, a Bible reader, was holding a service for a dead brother. Mary had to take part in these ceremonies, after which she was comfortably installed in her friend's house, and passed, for her, a comparatively quiet night, waking up quite recovered from her fever. The next day they paddled on into the utter wilds. The banks were inhabited by rare and beautiful birds and overgrown with varied flowering shrubs. She notes: 'Most luxurious, charming and pleasant trip this. The men are standing up swinging in rhythmic motion their long, rich, red wood paddles in perfect time to their elaborate, melancholy minor of exasperation with their cryptic complicated ways of communicating ideas with strings of cowries and pieces of leaf and stick. Only the other day I had to steer a course with a chart made of bits of plaintain leaf of different breadths denoting the villages I was to pass through.' [5]

Eight Years of Achievement

key boat song.' This entry is immediately followed by 'nearly lost with all hands' owing to the canoe upsetting on a sandbank close to deep water. Mary is undoubtedly fond of reminding her reader of the brevity of human joys.

They soon turned into a river which Mary calls by its native name, the Karkola—a river then entered on no map, and on which no white person had travelled. Ahead of them now lay 'all Fan' country—and these Fans were said to be at war with one another, and all approaches dangerous. The safety of the party now depended on whether a certain trade friend of one of the crew would be found at the Fan village on Lake N'covi, to which they were bound. The lake, 'lovely, strangely melancholy, and lonely looking' was felt by them all to be also curiously sinister and repellent. It was certainly very nearly fatal for them. As they came near to the village a 'brown mass of naked humanity came pouring down' to face them. 'I must say', Mary writes, 'that never—even in a picture book—have I seen such a set of wild wicked-looking savages as those we faced that night, and with whom it was touch-and-go for twenty of the longest minutes I have ever lived, whether we fought—for our lives, I was going to say, but it would not have been even for that, but merely for the price of them.' At last among the angry faces two of Mary's crew recognized their friend, and cried out in an agony of fervent friendship, 'Don't you know me, my beloved Kiva?' Kiva did and they were saved. The reader is struck by the astonishing sequel to this grim scene, the polite introduction of Kiva to Mary, and a shaking of hands. They were then led up into the town where Mary's white face terrified the children. The town was 'exceedingly filthy—the remains of the crocodile they had been eating the week before last and piles of fish offal, and remains of an elephant, hippo or manatee—I really can't say which, decomposition was too far advanced—united to form a most impressive stench'. She was given a dirty little hut for her

The Second Journey: 'Going for Bush'

accommodation; and immediately started to negotiate for carriers and guides for the next stage of the journey, which would be mainly overland. The 'palaver' on this subject went on for hours; and when Mary tried to intervene she was told by one of her men that a price palaver of this kind could easily last for weeks. She would have none of this—and alone in this den of savages she had it given out 'my price is for a start tomorrow—after then I have no price—after that I go away'. She won. Kiva and two other important and stalwart citizens offered to go with her themselves, and very good company she was to find them.

The inhabitants, tired with talking and staring, settled down for the night. Mary lay in her hut on a wooden plank, where she was soon attacked by lice and mosquitoes. Even so, one would have expected her, after the adventures of the evening, to stay safely indoors, with one of her crew sleeping across her door for protection. But the minor horrors of West Africa were what upset her most. Besides, it was a fine starlit night. She stepped over the sleeping Ajumba, who was busy 'talking palaver' in his sleep, and went down to the shore of the lake. She slid a small Fan canoe into the water and paddled out.

'It was a wonderfully lovely quiet night with no light save that from the stars. One immense planet shone pre-eminent in the purple sky, throwing a golden path down on to the still waters. Quantities of big fish sprung out of the water, their glistening silver-white scales flashing so that they looked like slashing swords. Some bird was making a long, low booming sound away on the forest shore. I paddled leisurely across the lake to the shore on the right, and seeing crawling on the ground some large glow-worms, drove the canoe on to the bank among some hippo grass, and got out to get them.

'While engaged on this hunt I felt the earth quiver under

Eight Years of Achievement

my feet, and heard a soft big soughing sound, and looking round saw I had dropped in on a hippo banquet. I made out five of the immense brutes round me, so I softly returned to the canoe and shoved off, stealing along the bank, paddling under water, until I deemed it safe to run out across the lake for my island. I reached the other end of it to that on which the village is situated; and finding a miniature rocky bay with a soft patch of sand and no hippo grass, the incidents of the Fan hut suggested the advisability of a bath—. . . it would be a long time before I got another chance. . . . Carefully investigating the neighbourhood to make certain there was no human habitation near, I then indulged in a wash in peace. . . . While I was finishing my toilet I saw a strange thing happen. Down through the forest on the lake bank opposite came a violet ball the size of an orange. When it reached the sand beach it hovered along it to and fro close to the ground. In a few minutes another ball of similarly coloured light came towards it from behind one of the islets, and the two wavered to and fro over the beach, sometimes circling round each other. I made off towards them in the canoe, thinking—as I still do—they were some brand new kind of luminous insect. When I got on to their beach one of them went off into the bushes and the other away over the water. I followed in the canoe, for the water here is very deep, and, when I almost thought I had got it, it went down into the water and I could see it glowing as it sank until it vanished in the depths. I made my way back hastily, fearing my absence with the canoe might give rise, if discovered, to trouble, and by 3.30 I was back in the hut safe, but not so comfortable as I had been on the lake. A little before five my men are stirring and I get my tea. I do not state my escapade to them, but ask what those lights were. "Akom," said the Fan, and pointing to where I had been said, "they came there—it was an Aku"—or bush devil. More than ever did I regret not having secured one of those sort of pheno-

The Second Journey: 'Going for Bush'

mena. What a joy a real devil, appropriately put up in raw alcohol, would have been to my scientific friends!'

Mary was a careful and accurate observer, and there can be no doubt that she did see this violet apparition—its real nature may be still a mystery.

The next morning her boatload set off accompanied by those distinguished Fan citizens, Kiva, Fika and Wiki, in a separate canoe. On the shore of a small lake communicating with Lake N'covi they left their canoes and started on the cross-country journey. It was a desperate journey, all things natural, human and sub-human conspiring against them. The way led over and through long slopes of fallen timber and deep bogs; the few African settlements were known to be on the war-path against one another. The three Fans, accustomed to the forest, strode on over fallen trees and rocks with an easy graceful stride. Mary's company trailed after. Somewhat ambiguously she remarks: 'What saved us weaklings was the Fans' appetites; every two hours they sat down, and had a snack.' On these occasions she seems to have rested hardly at all, but to have taken advantage of the halt to go ahead by herself. It was little short of miraculous that after long years of a confined domestic life she should have had the physical power to keep up with these Africans and in several cases to out-do them. When a dangerous swamp had to be forded she took her turn in the lead; and once when the only way across a deep ravine was over a narrow tree-trunk she alone decided to cross by the tree; the others preferred to force their way through the torrent. Mary had not the strength to fight the torrent, and took the over-head route. 'If only the wretched thing had had its bark on it would have been better, but it was bare, bald, and round, and a slip meant death on the rocks below. I rushed it and reached the other side in safety.' There are certainly some traits in human nature which are quite universal: when she

Eight Years of Achievement

reached the other side her company declared that they had gone through the water just to wash their feet.

It appears that Mary did in fact traverse this thick jungle and these swamps in a skirt; for it was during this march that she fell into the spike-lined game-trap, and was protected by her draperies.

This trap was an indication that they were nearing the Fan village of Efoua. Only Kiva had ever been to Efoua before, and no one felt confident that they would not all 'spend the evening at Efoua simmering in cooking pots'. The party were fortunate; most of the local men were away on an elephant hunt, and two of the Fans found acquaintances in the village. Altogether Mary was pleased with Efoua—it was much cleaner than most Fan towns, and she quickly made friends with the two chiefs, in the house of one of whom she spent the night. It was, like most of her West African nights, disturbed—this time by a smell. Waking up after a brief doze she 'noticed the smell in the hut was violent . . . and had an unmistakably organic origin'. Knocking the ash end off the smouldering bush-light that lay burning on the floor, she investigated, and tracked the smell to some bags hanging against the wall. We now discover from her account of what happened that she also travelled with a hat—and here is how she used it on this occasion.* Taking down the biggest bag 'I carefully noted how the tie-tie had been put round its mouth; for these things are important and often mean a lot. I then shook its contents out in my hat, for fear of losing anything of value. They were a human hand, three big toes, four eyes, two ears, and other portions of the human frame. The hand was fresh, the others only so so, and shrivelled.' It was later explained to Mary by Wiki that the Fans when they eat friendly tribes-folk like to keep a little something as a memento.

---

* The sealskin cap which she wore on her travels can be seen, and in excellent condition, at the Royal Geographical Society.

The Second Journey: 'Going for Bush'

After a breath of fresh air through the door, she went to sleep. The next day she parted on the most friendly terms with the two chiefs 'with many expressions of hope on both sides that we should meet again'.

She was undoubtedly a social success with cannibals, and her own three Fan carriers were anxious for her to stay 'in this delightful locality'. At the next village she gave them more reason than her charm for valuing her company.

This village was called Egaja, and had the worst reputation among the Fans of any in the region. 'When the first burst of Egaja conversation began to boil down into something reasonable, I found that a villainous-looking scoundrel, smeared with soot and draped in a fragment of antique cloth, was a head chief in mourning.' But by and by another chief arrived. 'I saw at once he was a very superior man to any of the chiefs I had yet met with; it was not his attire, remarkable though that was for the district, for it consisted of a gentleman's black frock coat such as is given in the ivory bundle, a bright blue felt sombrero hat, and ample cloth of Boma check; but his face and general bearing was distinctive, and very powerful and intelligent. . . . He was exceedingly courteous.' Mary decided to put this man on his best behaviour by boldly telling him what a bad name Egaja had as 'a thief town'. It was a risky proceeding, but it worked. To realize just how bold it was one must remember that not only had these tribes never seen a white man, but they were not even in touch with any ordinary trade routes—passing such goods as they had along jungle tracks into the hands of other rather less remote African traders. Those who dealt direct with European factories had a good name to keep up—it was bad for business if you were liable to eat wandering traders and steal their goods. But isolated Africans in the bush cared nothing for the reputableness of their sources of supply. Mary could win some goodwill by the judicious distribution of gifts—but her whole stock could have

Eight Years of Achievement

been stolen over the dead bodies of herself and her band, had things taken a wrong turn. There was really nothing but her personality to protect them all.

In this town she needed all her resources. First she was asked by the leading chief for medical advice for his old mother who was suffering with the most repulsive ulcers—much more repulsive Mary found them than the bag of mementoes she had examined in Efoua. She drained and disinfected and poulticed the ulcers, and the old lady fell comfortably asleep. Thereupon all the sick of Egaja turned up for pills and poultices. After a long session in surgery Mary retired for the night. An hour or two later there was a great commotion because one of the Fan carriers had been too attentive to an Egajan beauty. Mary paid damages and retired again to bed. But at four in the morning the whole village was in tumult, and the voice of Kiva was heard calling for help. 'I suggested to the Ajumba that they should go out; but no, they didn't care a row of pins if one of our Fans did get killed, so I went.' It transpired that Kiva had once appropriated an ivory tusk which belonged to a native of Egaja, and had never handed over the coat he had promised by way of payment. So the village had decided 'to foreclose forthwith on the debtor's estate, and as the estate was represented by Kiva's person, to take and seize upon it and eat it'. She comments:

'It is always highly interesting to observe the germ of any of our own institutions existing in the culture of a lower race. Nevertheless it is trying to be hauled out of one's sleep in the middle of the night and plunged into this study. Evidently this was a trace of an early form of the Bankruptcy Court; the Court which clears a man of his debt being represented by the knife and the cooking pot; the white-washing, as I believe it is termed with us, also shows, only it is not the debtor who is whitewashed but the creditors, doing themselves over with white

Canoe and jungle, Lagos Creeks

The Second Journey: 'Going for Bush'

clay to celebrate the removal of their enemy from his sphere of meretricious activity. This inversion may arise from the fact that white-washing a debtor who was about to be cooked would be unwise, as the stuff would boil off the bits and spoil the gravy. There is always some fragment of sound sense underlying African institutions. Kiva was, when I got out, tied up, talking nineteen to the dozen; and so was everyone else; and a lady was working up white clay in a pot.'

Mary's exhibition of medical skill had occurred just in time to save the situation. The villagers regarded her with respect; and the chief was her firm friend. After hours in which she played the part, she says, of a criminal lawyer for the defence, Kiva was bought off.

When day came she hurried her band out of Egaja as quickly as she could.

Occasionally the track led them through comparatively unencumbered forest where the cool shade was a blessed relief. Here Mary was able to observe the grand and grim battle of tropical vegetation.

'The character of the whole forest was very interesting. Sometimes for hours we passed among thousands upon thousands of grey-white columns of uniform height (about a hundred to a hundred and fifty feet); at the top of these the boughs branched out and interlaced among each other, forming a canopy or ceiling, which dimmed the light even of the equatorial sun to such an extent that no undergrowth could thrive in the gloom. The statement of the struggle for existence was published here in plain figures, but it was not, as in our climate, a struggle against climate mainly, but an internecine war from over population. . . . Now and again we passed among vast stems of buttressed trees, sometimes enormous in girth; and from their far-away summits hung great bush ropes, some as straight as plumb lines, others coiled round, and intertwined

Eight Years of Achievement

among each other, until one could fancy one was looking on some mighty battle between armies of gigantic serpents. . . . I was very curious as to how they got up straight, and investigation showed me that many of them were carried up with a growing tree.

'Some stretches of this forest were made up of thin, spindly stemmed trees of great height, and among these stretches I always noticed the ruins of some forest giant, whose death by lightning, or by his superior height having given the demoniac tornado wind an extra grip on him, had allowed sunlight to penetrate the lower regions of the forest; and then evidently the seedlings and saplings, who had for years been living a half-starved life for light, shot up. They seemed to know that their one chance lay in getting with the greatest rapidity to the level of the top of the forest. No time to grow fat in the stem. No time to send out side branches or any of those vanities. Up, up to the light level, and he among them who reached it first won in this game of life or death; for when he gets there he spreads out his crown of upper branches and shuts out the life-giving sunshine from his competitors, who pale off and die, or remain dragging on an attenuated existence waiting for another chance, and waiting sometimes for centuries.'

Thus came about those easier tracks, that cool twilight—'those lovely stretches of forest, gloomy down below, but giving hints that far away above us was a world of bloom and scent and beauty which we saw as much as earth-worms a flower-bed. Here and there the ground was strewn with great cast blossoms, thick, wax-like, glorious cups of orange and crimson and pure white, each one of which was in itself a handful, and which told us that some of the trees above us were showing a glory of colour to heaven alone.'

At last they came upon a little river which was running, as the compass showed, not southwards like all the others they

The Second Journey: 'Going for Bush'

had crossed, but north-west, towards the Rembwé. They had crossed the watershed.

Many other adventures and narrow escapes occurred before they reached the Rembwé and the trade station there, where Mary could pay off her Fans in goods. This process she found extremely amusing, though she was still in some personal danger, since even now she was not in touch with any European trader, and it was essential for her to satisfy her carriers. Everything was settled amicably in the end. 'We started talking trade, with my band in the middle of the street; making a patch of uproar in the moonlit surrounding silence. As soon as we thought we had got one gentleman's mind settled as to what goods he would take his pay in, and were proceeding to investigate another gentleman's little fancies, gentleman number one's mind came all to pieces again, and he wanted to "room his bundle", i.e. change articles in it for other articles of an equivalent value, if it must be, but of a higher if possible. Oh ye shopkeepers in England who grumble at your lady customers, just you come out here and try to serve, and satisfy a set of Fans!'

The troop was disbanded, the Ajumbas going back with the Fans with whom they seem to have been at last on friendly terms. Mary herself had what she calls a touching farewell with the Fans, those ' "terrible M'pongwe" whom I hope to meet with again'.*

When she reached civilization at Glass in Gaboon river she was in hopes of avoiding Mr Hudson, for she knew that 'since he had deposited me in safe hands with Mme Jacot, with many injunctions to be careful, there were many incidents in my career that would not meet with his approval'. But he was on the pier waiting for her, having already sent a surf-boat up the Rembwé to look for her. He had heard something of her

* The M'pongwe and the Fans are kindred tribes, and Mary here uses the phrase 'terrible M'pongwe' to describe the cannibal branch.

Eight Years of Achievement

'goings on'. He did not approve. Mary tried in vain to explain to him how much she had enjoyed herself.

Mr Hudson thought that Miss Kingsley's escapades were suicidal, and that only the most unaccountable good luck had brought her and her followers back alive. Are we to arrive at the same conclusion? Surely not. It was not luck which enabled her to overcome great natural obstacles, and to pacify and control the wildest and most unscrupulous savage tribes—it was above all stark intelligence. When she met wild animals in the forest, or when it was necessary to ford a deep and treacherous swamp, her acute powers of observation and memory aided her natural judgement; she chose the best method of dealing with the danger. Among the Fans her practical knowledge, for example of medicine, and her extraordinary insight into their primitive minds and their customs gave her the power she needed and created conditions in which her indomitable courage could be made effective. In a passage of *Travels in West Africa* she describes her pleasure in reading of mountaineering exploits among precipices and arêtes, and says that nothing on earth would persuade her to do these things herself: 'but they remind me of bits of country I have been through where you walk along a narrow line of security with gulfs of murder looming on each side, and where in exactly the same way you are as safe as if you were in your easy chair at home, as long as you get sufficient holding ground: not on rock in the bush village inhabited by murderous cannibals but on ideas in these men's and women's minds; and these ideas, which I think I may say you will always find, give you safety. It is not advisable to play with them, or to attempt to eradicate them, because you regard them as superstitious; and never, never shoot too soon. I have never had to shoot, and hope never to have to; because in such a situation one white alone with no troops to back him means a clean finish.' [6]

Though she felt it unladylike to go shooting innocent wild

The Second Journey: 'Going for Bush'

creatures, on the Rembwé expedition when she seems to have carried both a knife and a revolver she plainly would, if necessary, have sold her life dear and have shot some Africans in the process. To this readiness she attributes part of her popularity with the Fans. 'A certain sort of friendship', she says, 'soon arose between the Fans and me. We each recognized that we belonged to that same section of the human race with whom it is better to drink than to fight. We knew we would each have killed the other if sufficient inducement were offered, and so we took a certain amount of care that the inducement should not arise.'

It would have horrified the Victorian drawing-rooms, where she was always ill at ease, but it was useful among the Fans—this fighting spirit of a long line of Kingsleys brought to birth in a young woman who had had to spend most of her life carrying a duster.

5

Some Animals and a Mountain

Though Mary was a fighting Kingsley, she was also—it is part of the enigma of her character—a gentle-hearted woman, averse to causing suffering or destroying life. When she declared that she did not think it lady-like to go about shooting things, what she meant by lady-like was merciful. She says 'I am habitually kind to animals', and she showed this kindness even to the dangerous creatures she met in the jungle, creatures of which she was, she admits, terrified. She never seems to have lost entirely, in any encounter with man or beast, a feeling of pity for a struggling fellow creature—a pity that could be stronger than fear.

She is said to have told Mrs Macmillan that she was once so distressed by the cries of a leopard caught in a trap that she went out in the middle of the night and set it free.[1] When it bounded out of the pit it stood glaring and sniffing at her, and no doubt she had that salt taste in her mouth. But she stood still and said firmly: 'Go home, you fool!' and the leopard went. On the face of it, it would seem rather unlikely that Mary would have endangered the lives of the natives, and her own reputation among them, by breaking open one of their traps. It is however entirely convincing that finding herself in close proximity with a leopard which had broken out of a trap, she should have said 'Go home, you fool', and it should have quickly gone. There was something about her at once

Some Animals and a Mountain

commanding and pacifying which both men and animals obeyed.

Many passages in her travel books tell of encounters with animals; sometimes she went with hunters, quite often she came across wild beasts when she was alone. The only animals which filled her with disgust as well as fear were gorillas. In a note to the *Travels* she writes:

'I have no hesitation in saying that the gorilla is the most horrible wild animal I have seen. I have seen at close quarters specimens of the most important big game of Central Africa, and with the exception of snakes, I have run away from all of them; but although elephants, leopards, and pythons give you a feeling of alarm, they do not give that feeling of horrible disgust that an old gorilla gives on account of its hideousness of appearance.'

Yet even for gorillas she felt admiration: 'Never have I seen anything to equal gorillas going through bush; it is a graceful, powerful, superbly perfect hand-trapeze performance.'

In many parts of Africa leopards are regarded with superstitious awe and associated with secret societies. Mary says:

'The ju-ju part of the leopard are the whiskers . . . gay reckless young hunters wear them stuck in their hair and swagger tremendously. . . . I really think that, taken as a whole, he is the most lovely animal I have ever seen; only seeing him, in the one way you can gain an idea of his beauty, namely in his native forest, is not an unmixed joy to a person, like myself, of a nervous disposition.'

She then relates an astonishing adventure, when alone in the jungle she crouched cheek by jowl with a leopard watching a tornado violent enough to paralyse them both:

'I had got caught in a tornado in a dense forest. The massive, mighty trees were waving like a wheatfield in an autumn gale

Eight Years of Achievement

in England.... The great trees creaked and groaned and strained against it and their bush-rope cables strained and smacked like whips, and ever and anon a thundering crash with snaps like pistol shots told that they and their mighty tree had strained and struggled in vain. The fierce rain came in a roar, tearing to shreds the leaves and blossoms and deluging everything.... Climbing up over a lot of rocks out of a gully bottom where I had been half drowned in a stream, and getting my head to the level of a block of rock, I observed right in front of my eyes, broadside on, maybe a yard off, certainly not more, a big leopard. He was crouching on the ground, with his magnificent head thrown back and his eyes shut. His forepaws were spread out in front of him and he lashed the ground with his tail, and I grieve to say, in face of that awful danger—I don't mean me, but the tornado—that depraved creature swore, softly, but repeatedly and profoundly. I did not get all these facts up in one glance, for no sooner did I see him than I ducked under the rocks, and remembered thankfully that leopards are said to have no power of smell. But I heard his observations on the weather, and the flip-flap of his tail on the ground. Every now and then I cautiously took a look at him with one eye round a rock-edge, and he remained in the same position. My feelings tell me he remained there twelve months, but my calmer judgement puts the time down at twenty minutes; and at last, on taking another cautious peep, I saw he was gone.... He had moved off in one of those weird lulls which you get in a tornado.'

She continues:

'It was an immense pleasure to have seen the great creature like that. He was so evidently enraged and baffled by the uproar and dazzled by the floods of lightning that swept down into the deepest recesses of the forest, showing at one second every detail of twig, leaf, branch, and stone round you, and

Some Animals and a Mountain

then leaving you in a sort of swirling dark until the next flash came; this and the great conglomerate roar of the wind, rain and thunder, was enough to bewilder any living thing.' [2]

The extraordinary detachment of which she was capable is shown by this comment on her adventure. That she was able to notice and to remember afterwards with a feeling of pleasure, the beauty of an animal, under such circumstances, is wholly characteristic. She seems hardly ever to have been so frightened or so acutely uncomfortable as to be unable to observe, to be amused, or to admire.

'I have never hurt a leopard intentionally.' There was however one occasion when she did astonish one intentionally. She had been roused in the night by what she thought was a frantic dog fight in an adjoining hut, where a boar-hound had a litter. She went to deal with the situation—'a whirling mass of animal matter'; but after she had hurled a stool or two, 'the meeting broke up into a leopard and a dog. The leopard crouched, I think to spring at me. I can see its great, beautiful, lambent eyes still, and I seized an earthen water-cooler and flung it straight at them. It was a noble shot; it burst on the leopard's head like a shell and the leopard went for bush one time. Twenty minutes after people began to drop in cautiously and inquire if anything was the matter.'

One of her most alarming adventures with wild animals, but one where the men were more alarming than the beasts, was related in the last lecture she gave, to the Imperial Institute, in February 1900 (it is reprinted in the second edition of *West African Studies*). She had been speaking of African Secret Societies, and of how easy it is to make mistakes when you are studying them—a study which is in any case highly dangerous.

'The most terrifying mistake I ever made, I made when I was pottering about Mount Njawki, beetle-hunting, etc. One afternoon when walking down a bush path alone, I found

Eight Years of Achievement

myself facing on a little open space, seven men all got up in the most extraordinary costumes imaginable.... My heart went into my mouth and my mind went into my heels, for, oh! thinks I, here's one of those precious men's secret societies in full session. I knew that it was death for an uninitiated native man or any native woman to see such a thing; what it might be for me, I did not know—I did not want to. I executed what I thought was a masterly retreat, full of the hope that as they all seemed sitting sound asleep, they had not seen me. I soon heard the phit-phat of a man's running feet coming after me, and knew retreat was no good.'

Without speaking a word the man beckoned to her to follow him, and led her back to the others. She was forced to accompany them through the forest, nobody saying a word, but uttering strange cries and melancholy whines and howls. After walking on for a mile or so her companions sat down, and she remained leaning against a tree; wishing, she says, that Professor Kohler of Berlin, Professor Tylor, Professor Frazer and all the other distinguished anthropologists could be there to study this interesting secret society, and not she. But in the end, after a fearful period of suspense for Mary, it turned out that it was not a secret society; they were on a monkey hunt. Their purpose was by making themselves look 'uncommon queer' to arouse the intense curiosity which no monkey can long resist. The men sat still, and in due course down came the monkeys, 'clinging to each other for better protection, intent on investigation'. The men then drew out their arrows and shot several of them.

'Then my companions threw off their fancy dresses and explained that they could not speak before because it would have given the whole show away—monkeys, according to them, well knowing a human language, and success depending on our party not being taken for human; and they further

Some Animals and a Mountain

explained, I am sure with no uncivil intention, that as I was quite the very queerest object they had personally ever seen, they thought I was a heaven-sent addition to a monkey hunt. Well, if I had known that earlier, I might have spent a more comfortable afternoon.'

'I don't mention half my picnics in the *Travels*', she told a friend. But of her last she gives the full story as written down at the time in her diary.[3] She was already on her way home, having left the French Congo with much regret, and intending only a short stay in Cameroon River where the S.S. *Niger* was calling.

'From the deck of the *Niger* I found myself again confronted with my great temptation—the magnificent Mungo Mah Lobeh—the Throne of Thunder. Now it is none of my business to go up mountains. There's next to no fish on them in West Africa, and precious little good rank fetish, as the population on them is sparse—the African, like myself, abhorring cool air. Nevertheless, I feel quite sure that no white man has ever looked on the great Peak of Cameroon without a desire arising in his mind to ascend it and know in detail the highest point on the western side of the continent, and indeed one of the highest points in all Africa.'

Mary tells us that she was afraid of mountaineering; a very good reason, for her, for putting herself to the test. But the strongest challenge came from the mountain's sheer beauty. The great peak rises up out of the sea to a height of 13,760 feet.

'Every time you pass it by its beauty grows on you with greater and greater force, though it is never twice the same. Sometimes it is wreathed with indigo black tornado clouds, sometimes crested with snow, sometimes softly gorgeous with gold, green and rose-coloured vapours tinted by the setting sun, sometimes completely swathed in dense cloud so that

Eight Years of Achievement

you cannot see it at all; but when you once know it is there it is all the same, and you bow down and worship.'

This final picnic was less dangerous than many of her adventures, but risks from hurricanes, mists, precipices and lost tracks were considerable; as usual efforts were made to dissuade her, and as usual in vain. She elected to ascend from the south-east and it eventually proved that she was the first person ever to do so. Several Germans and one or two Englishmen had climbed it from the other side. She apparently chose the south-east because she had hopes of getting a view of certain uncharted mountain ranges from that side. The band of Africans who accompanied her were not in themselves so dangerous as her cannibal escorts; but being coast-dwellers they lacked the toughness and the skills of the natives of the bush. Their softness and lack of initiative were in themselves a danger, and in the end Mary had to do the last part of the ascent alone.

The general unco-operativeness of her band was partly due to a feeling among them that it was unwise, because it was impertinent, to flout the Throne of Thunder by climbing up it. To most Africans, as she explains in *West African Studies*, the spirit of man is a very humble spirit in comparison with those of mountain and rapid and surf and storm. These powerful spirits have their 'politics',

'and private matters of these very great people are things the human being had better keep out of; and it is advisable for him to turn his attention to making terms with them and go into their presence with his petition when their own affairs are prosperous, when their tempers are not up over some private ultra-human affair of their own. I well remember the opinions expressed by my companions regarding the folly—mine of course—of obtruding ourselves on Mungo when that noble mountain was vexed too much.' [4]

It was in fact the wrong season for obtruding on Mungo—

Some Animals and a Mountain

it was the tornado season—but then, Mary explains, she had no choice; it was now or never.

Her company consisted of some porters, a cook—a worthy man, but one who, after the manner of cooks, occasionally gave her notice when the going was extra bad; one named Kefalla whose chief contribution was to lecture everyone else on matters relevant and irrelevant; a headman with the name of Bum; one called Monrovia Boy, who proved one of the most trustworthy of the band; and an active and loyal, though slightly crazy man called Xenia.

It was some time before Mary detected that her company had agreed among themselves to compel her, by one dodge or another, to abandon the excursion. They did not realize that such methods, with this particular 'Ma', would not work.

They started on 20 September 1895, in fine weather, with lovely views of the foothills of the mountain, the soil and vegetation brilliant with rich colour. They followed a road which was being made by a German engineer, but only half a mile of it was finished and the rest was an intractable mass of broken rock and blasted tree-trunks. Soon it began to rain and continued till the track and the trackers were running with water. But there was always something worth while for Mary to see. When to their relief they left the road and turned into a forest path:

'We seem to be in a ghost-land forest, for the great palms and red-woods rise up into the mist before us, and fade out in the mist behind as we pass on. The rocks which edge and strew the path at our feet are covered with exquisite ferns and mosses—all the most delicate shades of green imaginable, and here and there of absolute gold colour, looking as if some ray of sunshine had lingered too long playing on the earth, and had got shut off from heaven by the mist, and so lay nestling among the rocks until it might rejoin the sun.'

Eight Years of Achievement

Late in the afternoon they reached 'the hut of a Basel Mission black Bible-reader', and here Mary agreed to stop for the night. After food and some rum all round, she settled down, hoping to get warm and to sleep. But she was soon aroused, as so often on her journeys, by 'enterprising sight-seers pushing open the window shutters; when I look round there are a mass of black heads sticking through the window-hole'. After a while she lights a candle and reads 'Günther on Fishes'.

'If this sort of weather goes on I expect I shall specialise fins and gills myself. Room becomes full of blacks. Unless you watch the door, you do not see how it is done. You look at a corner one minute and it is empty, and the next time you look that way it is full of rows of white teeth and watching eyes.'

When the eyes withdraw there are other disturbances:

'Vaseline the revolver. Wish those men would leave off chattering.... Evidently great jokes in next room.... The women of the village outside have been keeping up, this hour and more, a most melancholy coo-ooing. Those foolish creatures are evidently worrying about their husbands, who have gone down to market in Ambas Bay, and who, they think, are lost in the bush. I have not a shadow of doubt that those husbands who are not home by now are safely drunk in town.'

In the morning she is wakened by the sounds of one returned husband whacking his protesting wife. But the others none the less go on wistfully 'coo-ooing'.

The next day the climbers spent floundering on through torrents and mud slides and ceaseless rain. But as always there was much that was interesting and beautiful for the leader of the party to observe and enjoy; there were few fishes, but there were other zoological specimens.

'I have to pause in life's pleasures because I want to measure one of the large earthworms.... He was eleven inches and

Some Animals and a Mountain

threequarters. He detained me some time getting this information, because he was so nervous during the operation. . . .

'The country is gloriously lovely if one could only see it for the rain and mist; but one only gets dim hints of its beauty when some cold draughts of wind come down from the great mountains and seem to push open the mist-veil as with spirit hands, and then in a minute let it fall together again.'

In the evening they reached the village of Buea, a place only recently subdued and pacified by the German authorities; from here, as the mist cleared, the great crater wall of Mungo loomed up. 'It looks awfully steep when you know you have got to go up it.' They were welcomed by the German official, Herr Liebert, and were settling in, when down came a tornado, sending 'its lightning running over the ground in streams of living death. Oh, they are nice things, are tornadoes! I wonder what they will be like when we are up in their home; up atop of that precious wall?'

'September 22nd. Wake at five. Fine morning, fine view. . . . No one stirring till six, when people come out of their huts, and stretch themselves and proceed to begin the day, in the African's usual perfunctory, listless way. . . . My crew are worse than the rest.'

She announces that she is going on up, and obstruction begins. Kefalla arrives on the scene to protest: 'You no sabe this be Sunday, Ma?' The argument cuts no ice. Then Kefalla produces another reason—two of the boys are sick—with the usual 'tummick' trouble of the African, real or imaginary. Mary borrows two other labourers and a sergeant from her host, and the two sick men are sent home.

They presently entered thick dark forests, where for the first time Mary saw tree ferns growing in luxuriant profusion, but the track was soon lost or hopelessly blocked, and they had to return to their German friend who gave them fresh

Eight Years of Achievement

directions. The new track led into what Mary describes as an *Urwald*, wonderfully beautiful with flowers and ferns, but full also of snakes and scorpions. Mungo was by now beginning to brew a tornado, and the rain started again. When they emerged at the edge of the timber belt, the boys demanded a halt, and the setting up of camp for the night. That was all very well, but could they make a fire? Oh, no. Unlike the Fans, for whose vigorous company Mary often longed on this excursion, they had no idea how a fire could be made without matches. 'They are coast boys, all of them, and therefore used to luxury.' It was astonishing that the Africans in this region had so soon lost their native skills, and Mary's experience with these men confirmed her opinion of the harmful effects of European life on the coast. During the following few days she had to teach them much of her own bush-lore; how to make fires in pouring rain, how to level a camping ground, and erect wind-screens.

Leaving her men in camp Mary then went out, during a bright period of twilight, to take compass bearings and prospect for the next day's climb up the mountain wall. Soon her men 'who have missed their "Ma", are yelling for her dismally'. But by the time she got back they were wildly cheerful, having succeeded, while the cook was busy feeding, in broaching the stock of rum. Finally they sang and quarrelled themselves to sleep.

'I write by the light of an insect-haunted lantern, sitting on the bed, which is tucked away among the trees some twenty yards away from the boys' fire. There is a bird whistling in a deep rich note that I have never heard before.'

The next morning in fine weather she set out taking six of the men with her. Fortune seemed to be smiling. But there was soon a halt while some of the boys searched for a spring of water and found none. It now transpired that there was no

Peaks of Cameroons mountain (from Burton's *Abeokuta and the Camaroons Mountains*, 1863)

Cameroons mountain in eruption, 1954

Some Animals and a Mountain

water, either with the advance party or in the camp, and none to be found on the mountain.

'This means failure unless tackled, and it is evidently a trick played on me by the boys, who intentionally failed to let me know of this want of water before leaving Buea. Now they evidently think that there is nothing to be done but to return to Buea, and go down to Victoria, and get their pay, and live happily ever after, without having to face the horror of the upper regions of the mountain. They have worked their oracle with other white folk, I find, for they quote the other white folk's docile conduct as an example to me.'

She expressed her opinion vigorously of the other folk and of her own party and sent a man right back to the German station for a supply of water. Giving orders that the water was to be brought on to a camp which she would make at the top of the mountain wall, she left a sulky band of boys, and went ahead alone. But two boys, shamed into following, were seen toiling up after her—Xenia, the slightly mad, carrying her black bag. This was considerate of him, for it would, one feels, have been awkward to lose your hand-bag on the precipices of Mungo Mah Lobeh. The rocky ledges up which Mary climbed were, in sheltered places, thronged with shrubs and flowers, looking as if they had plenty to drink, but there was not a drop to slake her thirst. The sun was fierce, and a strong wind was blowing. When Xenia overtook her she found a little bottle of sour claret in the bag from which they had a sip; then Xenia sat down to rest; the other boy had already given up.

It was from vantage points on this part of the climb that she enjoyed the most rewarding views; and she was alone to enjoy them. Far below her she could see the Mission house at Buea, and beyond and below that stretches of forest, and below again the mangrove swamps of the Cameroons estuary.

'It is a very noble view, giving one an example of the peculiar

Eight Years of Achievement

beauty one oft-times gets in this West African scenery, namely colossal sweeps of colour. The mangrove swamps looked today like a vast damson-coloured carpet threaded with silver where the water ways ran.... After taking some careful compass bearings for future use regarding the Rumby and Omon range of mountains ... I turned my face to the wall of Mungo and continued the ascent. The sun, which was blazing, was reflected back from the rocks in scorching rays, but it was more bearable now, because its heat was tempered by a bitter wind.'

At the top of this great cliff she found herself on one edge of the vast crater of Mungo, with a number of taller peaks encircling it. Here she was exposed to the wind—'a wind that went through me, for I had been sweltering for nine months in equatorial swamps'. But the view from here was still more extensive, stretching far away towards the sea and Fernando Po. In one of the chasms of the mountain below a thunderstorm was brewing.

'Surely', she notes, 'Mungo Mah Lobeh himself, of all the thousands he annually turns out, never made one more lovely than this. Soon the white mists rose from the mangrove-swamp, and grew rose-colour in the light of the setting sun, as they swept upwards over the now purple high forests. In the heavens to the north there was a rainbow, vivid in colour, one arch of it going behind the peak, the other sinking into the mist sea below, and this mist sea rose and rose towards me, turning from pale rose colour to lavender, and where the shadow of Mungo lay across it, to a dull leaden grey. It was soon at my feet, blotting the under-world out, ... stretching in great spreading rivers over the crater plain, and then these coalescing everything was shut out save the two summits: that of Cameroon close to me, and that of Clarence away on Fernando Po. These two stood out alone, like great island masses made of iron rising from a formless silken sea. The space

Some Animals and a Mountain

around seemed boundless, and there was in it neither sound nor colour, nor anything with form, save those two terrific things. It was like a vision and it held me spell-bound, as I stood shivering on the rocks with the white mist round my knees, until into my wool-gathering mind came the memory of those anything but sublime men of mine; and I turned and scuttled off along the rocks like an agitated ant left alone in a dead universe.'

In the dusk, through the mist, having been short all day of food and water, Mary started down to collect her renegade band. She first picked up Xenia who was lost on his own and seemed rather crazier than usual. When at last she found the halting place of the morning the men had gone leaving an empty soda-water syphon, one of the only three the base camp possessed. By firing revolver shots which roused yells in reply, she finally located the camp, and there ensued a scene over which, she says, she draws a veil. 'They did not attempt to deny their desertion, but they attempted to explain it, each one saying that it was not he but the other boy who got fright too much.' She concludes her entry for that day by saying: 'I would not prevent those men of mine from going up that peak above me after their touching conduct today. Oh! no; not for worlds, dear things.'

But they didn't go—not all the way. Some of them, who complained of their 'tummicks', she sent back to Victoria. The water had not yet come; and with Kefalla, Xenia and Cook she had to wait in the forest camp till it at last arrived. There had also been a muddle over the food, and that too had to be waited for. Mary's face and lips were parched and bleeding from the sun and wind of the preceding day. The food arrived, and soon after a tornado, and the forest camp began to run with water. Kefalla started lecturing on the foolishness of mountaineering and the quantity of devils in this region.

Eight Years of Achievement

The next day, in the sopping wet camp, bundles were made up for the climb up the rock wall. Xenia, Bum, Monrovia Boy, Kefalla and a labourer from Buea made up the party. When they at last reached the top,

'the immense old crater floor before us is today the site of a seething storm, and the peak itself quite invisible. My boys are quite demoralised by the cold. I find most of them have sold the blankets I gave them out at Buea; and those who have not sold them have left them behind, from laziness perhaps, but more possibly from a confidence in their powers to prevent us getting so far.'

On the crater edge among some stunted trees they encamped and set fires going—all the while shivering in the bitter wind. 'Oh, Ma!' says Kefalla, 'it be cold, cold too much. Too much cold kill we black man, all same for one as too much sun kill you white man. Oh, Ma!' That night Mary decides to stay awake rather than huddle in a wet bed. She props herself against a tree, pretending to be asleep, and listens to a conversation between Kefalla and Xenia.

'I am rewarded by getting some interesting details, and form the opinion that both these worthies, in their pursuit of their particular ju-jus, have come into contact with white prejudices, and are now fugitives from religious persecution. I also observe they have both their own ideas of happiness. Kefalla holds it lies in a warm shirt. Xenia that it abides in warm trousers; and every half hour the former takes his shirt off, and holds it in the fire smoke, and then puts it hastily on; and Xenia, who is the one and only trouser wearer in our band, spends fifty per cent of the night on one leg struggling to get the other in or out of these garments, when they are either coming off to be warmed, or going on after warming.'

Leaning against her tree, sheltering a lantern under her blanket,

Some Animals and a Mountain

she makes her entries on the comic, charming and uncomfortable features of her surroundings.

'There seem but few insects here. I have only got two moths tonight—one pretty one with white wings with little red spots on, like an old-fashioned petticoat such as an early Victorian-age lady would have worn—the other a sweet thing in silver.'

'*September 26th.* The weather is undecided and so am I ... but I do not like to give up the peak after going through so much for it.'

She asks for volunteers, and the faithful Xenia and head man, Bum, announce their willingness to go with her. The steep climb to the highest peak is made harder by ridges of broken and crumbling rock. About two-thirds of the way up Xenia gives in. He is left wrapped in his blanket in a sheltered spot, and the other two go on.

'When we are some 600 feet higher the iron-grey mist comes curling and waving round the rocks above us, like some savage monster defending them from intruders, and I again debate whether I was justified in risking the men, for it is a risk for them at this low temperature, with the evil weather I know, and they do not know, is coming on. But still we have food and blankets with us enough for them, and the camp in the plain below they can reach all right if the worst comes to the worst; and for myself—well—that's my own affair, and no one will be a ha'porth the worse if I am dead in an hour. ... The head man decides to fail for the third time to reach the peak, and I leave him wrapped in his blanket with the bag of provisions, and go on alone into the wild grey, shifting, whirling mist above.'

When at last she reaches the summit, she has the luck of too many mountaineers: there is no view.

'Near the cairn on the ground are several bottles, some of

Eight Years of Achievement

which the energetic German officers, I suppose, had emptied in honour of their achievement, an achievement I bow down before, for their pluck and strength had taken them here in a shorter time by far than mine.' (They had however come the easier way, which Mary does not mention here.) 'The weather grows worse every minute, and no sign of any clearing shows in the indigo sky or the wind-reft mist. The rain lashes so fiercely I cannot turn my face to it and breathe, the wind is all I can do to stand up against. Verily I am no mountaineer, for there is in me no exultation, but only a deep disgust because the weather has robbed me of my main object in coming here, namely to get a good view and an idea of the way the unexplored mountain range behind Calabar trends. No doubt had the weather been clear I should have been able to do this well.'

Both skill and good luck must have attended Mary on her downward climb, over loose cinders and rotten lava, in a thick mist and lashing tropical wind and rain. She found and collected Bum and Xenia, and got safely back to the crater camp where there were fires and food. When the party had got warm and had been fed they went on that evening to the deserted and soaking forest camp. Here they spent the night, and on the next morning, after the usual series of misadventures, they got back to the German station at Buea. Seeing Mary utterly bedraggled and plastered with mud, the horrified Herr Liebert, once again as on her upward journey, offered her a bath. But one of the dangers this odd creature would not face under any circumstances was that of having a bath in an inadequately private bathroom—and Herr Liebert's had no proper doors or shutters. She washed off a little mud, and made up her mind not to arrive in Victoria that night till after dark.

She was to spend only a few more weeks in Africa, and the last entry in her Mungo diary makes a fitting close to her second and, as it proved, her last journey to the Coast.

Some Animals and a Mountain

'My men having all reported themselves safe I went to my comfortable rooms, but could not turn in, so fascinating was the warmth and beauty down there; and as I sat on the verandah overlooking Victoria and the sea, in the dim soft light of the stars, with the fire-flies round me, and the lights of Victoria away below, and heard the soft rush of the Lukala River, and the sound of the sea-surf on the rocks, and the tom-tomming and singing of the natives, all matching and mingling together, "Why did I come to Africa?" thought I. Why! who would not come to its twin brother hell itself for all the beauty and the charm of it!'

6

The 'Mind Forest'

When Mary reached Liverpool on 30 November 1895, she was met, to her surprise, by newspaper reporters. After the manner of reporters they seem to have asked her for her opinion on West Africa in a nutshell. She replied by passing over the many soaked and battered volumes of her diary and telling them they could find out from those. Articles in the leading newspapers and periodicals were soon busy with her exploits and with problems of West Africa usually much neglected. When she herself began to lecture and write, popular enthusiasm was further kindled by her originality, honesty and charm, as well as by the startling experiences she related in her off-hand way.

There were other kinds of recognition as well which she valued more. Scientists welcomed her collections of specimens—brought, heaven knows how, across rivers and jungles by cannibal carriers, carefully bottled and labelled. Her explorations of new territory greatly interested the geographers, and she was soon invited to lecture to scientific societies in different parts of the country. When her books appeared she won the approval she most desired, for many anthropologists greeted her studies of African culture as new and revealing. The noted anthropologist, Professor Tylor of Oxford, expressed a high opinion of her work, and said that no one had ever seen further into the mind of the Negro.

The 'Mind Forest'

It was this insight into the mind of the African which led to her being drawn, unwillingly and at great cost to herself, into the sphere of politics. Her political work must be discussed in a separate chapter. It is sixty years since she returned from her second journey, and during that time the political tide has flowed far, and in some directions which she would have deprecated; but what she saw in the 'mind forest' of the unsophisticated African is still interesting and important; and how she came to see so much is still a matter for astonishment.

She spent less than eighteen months in all in West Africa, and could only in that time gain a slight knowledge of some of the many native languages. Seasoned travellers warned her that she could expect to learn little about the obscure Fetish worship which she intended to study. She did in fact learn so much, through her ability to make friends with the Africans, that she became an authority on the subject. In his biography Stephen Gwynn writes: 'Those who are best qualified to judge are amazed by nothing so much as by the sort of divination through which she, without any adequate means of complete communication, arrived at the heart of conceptions foreign to the European mind. For the best qualified least dispute the accuracy of her conclusions: how she reached them without knowledge of the tongues is to them a mystery and a marvel.'

One explanation is certainly that these conceptions were less foreign to Mary's mind than to those of most of her European contemporaries. As for the language difficulties (and she mentions coming across one hundred and forty-seven different varieties!) her knowledge of what to expect and her natural shrewdness helped her to interpret, and to keep a check on her interpreters. Above all she will have been helped by the African's use of gesture. 'At least one third of African language', she writes, 'consists in gesture, and the gesture part is fairly common to all Tribes. The African's intelligence is far ahead of his language.... Some of them are very dependent on

Eight Years of Achievement

gesture. When I was with the Fans they frequently said "We will go to the fire so we can see what they say" when any question had to be decided after dark.'[1]

Mary on her side had traits which appealed to the Africans. She relished as they did the delights and subtleties of barter. Like them, melancholy underneath, she was merry on the surface, and could share their sense of fun. Even her collecting of specimens may well have appealed to the Fans. They too had their little bags full of preserved odds and ends—toes and fingers of dead friends or enemies; so why shouldn't she have her bottles of insects and fishes, carefully carried about whereever she went? Her being a woman does not seem to have troubled her cannibal friends. She was after all a white person and was therefore in a class apart; and she kept scrupulously to the best white man's traditions of justice and good faith.

She combined with a feminine impulse to help people who had much the matter with them, an open-minded scientific attitude which led her to look for root causes and to come slowly and cautiously to conclusions. In *Africa Dances* Mr Gorer expresses the view that by European standards West Africans must appear mad. Mary would have retorted that most of the human race are more or less mad, and that the madness of the African results in superstitious practices no worse than those of thirteenth-century Europe. She found him very primitive, but neither brutal nor unkindly in disposition; 'taken as a whole the gentlest kind of real human being that is made', and surrounded by vast problems of living which, with a rather poor equipment, he tried to solve as well as he could, and according to his lights. Those lights—whether of religion or philosophy—were dim for him; and in spite of her firm belief in God, to which she testifies in several of her letters, they were dim for her. She had thus infinite sympathy for people trying to come to terms with an existence so inexplicable and so dangerous. Only those who can accept a revealed

The 'Mind Forest'

religion could, she thought, have any sense of security. She was herself a pantheist, and found her surest guide to God from his works in nature. Her faith was sustained by her response to beauty—a response which she found wanting in the African, and by a trust in the power of goodness, which also he seemed to lack. To him everything is spiritual—but the spirits are as often bad as good, and there is no one to mediate between them, or between them and man. Perhaps at one time there had been, according to myths which Mary came across in Fernando Po. One of these told of a former state when the gods came freely down to help with mundane affairs. But there was a Fall—for which here again a woman was made responsible. Up the long, long ladder which connected heaven and earth and which the gods used, a cripple boy once started to climb. His mother, afraid of his falling, went up after him. 'The gods, horrified at the prospect of having boys and women invading heaven, threw down the ladder and have since left humanity severely alone.' [2]

Whether African culture reflects a decadence is perhaps still an open question. As Mary found the Africans, they appeared pathetically alone; without the stiffening traditions of remembered history, without the encouragement of legends of great ancestors, and without any sense that man was more important in the universe than the many other powerful and assertive spirits which surrounded him. The lack of any deified ancestors meant that there was no pattern of greatness for subsequent generations to emulate. Mary attributed the absence of hero-worship to conditions of life which did not produce heroic qualities—what Professor Toynbee might call absence of adequate challenge; a food supply obtainable without much effort; a warm enervating climate, and terrific uncontrollable natural phenomena. In any case, whatever heroic Africans might have existed they would probably have been forgotten, owing to what Mary calls the 'weak-mindedness of the African

Eight Years of Achievement

regarding time'. 'I am sure that you may place a limit of 500 years as the extreme one for the very oldest Negro or Bantu historical tradition.... The religious tradition may be of intense antiquity.' Children are educated in the cult of spirits, but no one would trouble to tell them 'that a chief of such and such a name once lived there where the Engombie-Gombie trees have been shadowed down again by the great forest. The chief is dead. The village is dead, "palaver done set", so the historical tradition fades out like smoke.' [3]

Seeing in everything a soul capable of acting as it chose, the African feels life to be mainly a matter of propitiating unseen forces, the spirit of the surf, tree spirits, animal spirits, human ghosts which even when they were members of your own family might make themselves very inconvenient if you had failed in your duty towards them either before or after death. On the other hand your dead relations might be a source of companionship. To the endless noise of the usual African village, the shouts over anything that was being done, the incessant conversation with others and with self, is added, Mary says, animated conversation with ghosts.[4] She once met a woman in a lonely bush path talking eagerly to some invisible person who was, it was explained, her dead mother.

Starting from this background of thought the African seemed to Mary to work out his plan for living very logically and carefully. She writes:

'The more you know the African, the more you study his laws and institutions, the more you recognise that the main characteristic of his intellect is logical, and you see how in all things he uses this sound but narrow thought-form. He is not a dreamer nor a doubter; everything is real, very real, horribly real to him... the quality of the African mind is strangely uniform.... It is this power of being able logically to account for everything that is, I believe, at the back of the tremendous permanency of Fetish in Africa.' [5]

The 'Mind Forest'

The philosophy behind Fetish could, Mary argues, be derived from the teachings of Spinoza—from the view that God was immanent in all his works. It was the African's misfortune that he applied this idea in such a clumsy and mechanical manner. Fetish worship involves the treating of any object in which a powerful spirit (sometimes called a ju-ju) is believed to be residing, with extreme respect and caution. To be on good terms with that spirit, by possessing or cherishing that object, is greatly to a man's advantage; it may bring him good fortune, or avert bad, and it may help him to harm his enemy. Witch men, medicine men, and priests usually possess many fetish objects, and are much feared and courted in consequence.

From this attitude to nature the idea arose, Mary writes, 'that death was always the consequence of the action of some malignant spirit'. A man may be killed by a person using a gun or arrow, but equally by that person enlisting the spirit of a tree to fall on his head, or of a rapid to upset his canoe.

'A man having thus gained a belief that there are more than human actors in life's tragedy, the idea that disease is also a manifestation of some invisible being's wrath and power, seems to me natural and easy.... He knows that you can get another man for a consideration to kill or harm a third party, and so he thinks he can also get, for a consideration, one of these superhuman beings to do so.'

Spirits that can be so employed have obviously nothing to do with what we mean by virtue.

'The orthodox Christian view of witchcraft contains in it an element not present in the West African affair; the Christian regards the witch with hatred as one knowing good but choosing evil. The West African has not this choice in his mind; he has to deal with spirits who are not, any of them, up to much in the way of virtue viewed from a human standpoint.' They may be 'downright bad if they get their tempers up or take a dislike

Eight Years of Achievement

to a man; there is not one of them beneficent to the human race at large'. 'The Fetish believer does not hold he lives in a state of sin, but that it is a thing he can commit now and then if he is fool enough. Sin to him is not what it is to us, a vile treason against a loving Father, but a very ill-advised act against powerful, nasty-tempered spirits.'

This kind of life picture presents few grounds for ethical principles of the European variety.

'The individual is supremely important to himself, and he values his friends and relations, but abstract affection for humanity at large, or belief in the sanctity of the lives of people with whom he is unrelated and unacquainted, the African barely possesses. He is only capable of feeling this abstract affection when under the influence of one of the great revealed religions which place the human being higher in the scale of Creation.'

It is interesting to remember in this connexion that at the present day, after all the years he has worked among the Africans, Dr Schweitzer finds difficulty in getting a patient in his hospital to help another if that other is a stranger and belonging to a different tribe.

Mary Kingsley was moved to pity by this isolation of the African, his sense of utter insecurity in regard to his fellows and to nature and the unseen world. The melancholy of his outlook affected even the children. Mary liked children, and she says that they always liked her. She must have observed the little Africans with close attention. In Appendix I to *Travels in West Africa* she writes:

'The black child is a very solemn thing. It comes into the world in large quantities and looks upon it with its great sad eyes as if it were weighing carefully the question whether or no it is a fit place for a respectable soul to abide in. Four times

The 'Mind Forest'

in ten it decides that it is not and dies. If, however, it decides to stay, it passes between two and three years in a grim and profound study—occasionally emitting howls which end suddenly in a sob—whine it never does. At the end of this period it takes to spoon food, walks about and makes itself handy to its mother or goes into the mission school. If it remains in the native state it has no toys of a frivolous nature, a little hoe or a little calabash are considered better training; if it goes into the school it picks up with astonishing rapidity the lessons taught it there—giving rise to hopes for its future which are only too frequently disappointed in a few years' time.'

Mary's pity for the African made her surprisingly tolerant of some of the worst barbarities resulting from his outlook. She saw his superstitions as at once the symptoms and the causes of fear, and she knew how easily fear leads to cruelty. On the human sacrifices made at the funerals of chiefs in the Calabar region she writes: 'The pathos of the thing, when you have grasped the underlying idea, is so deep that the strangeness of it passes away, and you almost forget to hate the horrors of the slaughter.'

In the African mind the dead are conceived as being at best in rather a bad way. The African does not indulge in any barbarous notions of hell fire, but he does think a live donkey is happier than a dead lion. So he feels it necessary to provide what comforts he can for his dead relatives, in the way of slaves and wives sent on to join them. He believes too that if you leave your dear departed too uncomfortable they may try to stage a come-back, and this can be most inconvenient.

Passing in her usual manner from the grim to the comic, Mary writes on the next page about the position of a new chief in relation to the dead one; 'particularly interesting have been their accounts of what the live chief says to the dead one'.

'Much of it, of course, is, for diplomatic reasons, not known

Eight Years of Achievement

outside official circles. But the general tone of these communications is well known to be of a nature to discourage the dead chief from returning, and to reconcile him to his existing state. Things are not what they were here. The price of oil is down, women are ten times more frivolous, slaves ten times more trying, white Consul men abound, also their guns are more deadly than of old . . . the whole country is going to the dogs, financially and domestically, in fact, and you are much better off where you are. Then come petitions for such help as the ghost chief and his ghost retinue can give.'

As Mary penetrated deeper into this 'mind forest' she became increasingly critical of those who were trying arbitrarily to root it out, without pausing to understand its nature or how it had grown up. At a time when psychology was only beginning to recognize the power and tenacity of inherited beliefs, she realized how impossible it was to civilize the African merely by telling him his beliefs were false, or evil; he must be civilized as far as possible *through* his own religion, not against it, and by encouraging all that was good in his own laws and customs.

'Find me', she once said in a lecture, 'a more cheerful set of human beings in this world than the West Africans who believe in Fetish; find me a region where crime for private greed is so rare, and then, not till then, will I say Fetish is a horrible thing.' [6] Her quarrel with the missions arose from their readiness to condemn African culture *in toto*, and to teach the native abstractions which he did not understand when they should have been teaching practical skills. They were, she feared, stocking Africa with bogus converts, and conceited, idle, black-coated blacks, who because they could read and write despised the rest of their countrymen. 'Inactivity in Africa is death.' What was most needed was technical instruction 'which by instilling into his mind ideas of discipline, and providing him with manual occupation, will save him from

The 'Mind Forest'

these relapses which are now the reproach of the missionary effort and the curse and degradation of the African'.[7] It was among the untaught bushmen that she more often found honesty and decent principles and just laws, especially in relation to land and other property; among the sophisticated natives of the coast these good qualities were 'discernible mainly by their absence'.

Undoubtedly the African who could genuinely accept Christianity had crossed a great gulf—from a god-forsaken into a god-cherished existence. As some of these converts said to Mary: 'It does a man good to know God loves him; it makes him proud too much.' But with her keen eye for humbug she detected that most so-called converts were nothing of the kind. 'A really converted African', she writes, 'is a very beautiful form of Christian; but those Africans who are the mainstay of missionary reports . . . have merely had the restraint of fear removed from their minds in the mission schools without the greater restraint of love being put in its place.'[8] The average African goes to mission schools, she says, 'only to learn what he calls "sense", i.e. white man's ways and language, which will enable him to trade with greater advantage'.[9]

In Mary's opinion there were two obvious reasons why the converted Negro so often relapsed. One reason related to the conduct of the white man, and the other to that of the white man's God. The African was sure to feel in time that—from a practical point of view, and he had almost no other—the white God was no more help than Fetish gods when calamity descended.

'I know no more distressing thing than to see an African convert brought face to face with that awful thing we are used to, the problem of an omnipotent God and a suffering world. This does not worry the African convert until it hits him personally in grief and misery. When it does, and he

Eight Years of Achievement

turns and calls upon the God he has been taught will listen, pity and answer, his use of what the scoffers at the converted African call "catch phrases" is horribly heart-rending to me ... and I see the temptation to return to those old gods—the gods from whom he never expected pity, presided over by a god that does not care. All that he had to do with them was not to irritate them, to propitiate them, to buy their services when wanted, and above all to dodge and avoid them, while he fought it out and managed devils at large.' [10]

Another thing which weakened the hold of Christian teaching on the African mind was, Mary held, the curiously malleable nature of the average European conscience.

'There are many who will question whether conscience is a sufficiently large factor in an African mind for us to think of taking it into account; but whether you call it conscience, or religious bent, or fear, the factor is a large one. An African cannot say, as so many Europeans evidently easily can, "Oh, that is all right from a religious point of view, but one must be practical you know"; and it is this factor which makes me respect the African deeply and sympathise with him, for I have this same unmanageable hindersome thing in my own mind, which you can call anything you like; I myself call it honour. Now conscience when conditioned by Christianity is an exceedingly difficult thing for a trader to manage satisfactorily to himself. A mass of compromises have to be made with the world, and a man who is always making compromises gets either sick of them or sick of the thing that keeps on nagging at him about them, or he becomes merely gaseous-minded about them all round.' [11]

Whatever the evils of Fetish worship, it seems to have proved, as Mary would have anticipated, almost ineradicable. Her wide knowledge of West African history showed her how little African culture had seemed able to change under the spas-

The 'Mind Forest'

modic influences of Europe. In *West African Studies*, speaking of the long periods, from Egyptian times on, when African exploration was in abeyance, she writes:

'Whenever the white man has settled down with his home affairs and has had time to spare, he has always gone and looked up the African again, "discovered him", and he has always found him in the same state of culture that the pioneers of the previous Bluth-period found him in. Hanno does not find down the West Coast another Carthage—he finds bush fires, and hears the tom-tom and the horns and the shouts. He finds people slightly clad and savage. Then read Aluise da Ca da Mostro and the rest of Prince Henry's adventures; well, you might—save that the old traveller is more interesting—almost be reading a book published yesterday. The only radical change made for large quantities of Africans by means of white intercourse was made by exporting them to America. How this is going to turn out we do not yet know.' [12]

Recently it has seemed not only that Fetish worship is ineradicable but that it tends to survive in its worse forms. Some authorities on West Africa report that witchcraft is today on the increase; and we have some unfortunate examples of a type of African who attends our universities, appears highly civilized, and returns home to encourage and indulge in the most barbarous practices and beliefs. Mary relates an instance of this kind of relapse in a letter to her cousin Rose Kingsley, written from Calabar in 1895.

'The pet example of what Christianity and civilization can do for a negro was a native who was brought up and educated at a college in England and who has not long returned to his native shore; so resplendent on his return in store clothes, patent leather boots and high hat, that his native shore hardly knew him. This man—whose cabinet-sized photograph has decorated many a Missionary album, and been shown round

Eight Years of Achievement

at meetings, was seen by the authorities dancing denude of all coverings save a little touch of white paint, with a human hand freshly hewn off its original owner tied onto each of his wrists, human feet on each ankle, and another foot he held by the great toe in his teeth while he danced his dance of his own particular devil.' [13]

Though Mary defended some aspects of Fetish, she realized that the great need of the African was for a faith which could raise him in his own esteem. She thought the spread of Islam in Africa was partly due to its being a less exacting faith than Christianity (more manageable for the trader's conscience) while at the same time treating man as paramount in creation. It is, she says, 'pleasanter than Fetish, where a man in company with a host of spirits is fighting for his own hand before the gods eternally'.

Darkest Africa is perhaps as much a product of man's thinking as of nature's struggles and violences. Mary refers on several occasions to the terrible melancholy which African religion can generate. Writing to a Cambridge friend from Calabar in 1895, she says:

'The malignant melancholy these Africans suffer from is very strange. You would think with their happy-go-lucky indifferentism, their want of the deeper passions, or interest in facts underlying life, and the ease of their physical conditions, they would be the last people to suffer from *weltschmertz*, but every now and again they seem to get a glimpse behind the veil and turn sick with the horror of it and kill themselves. When you question them about it, all you can get out of them is "I no fit to live", and off they start hanging themselves and cutting their throats all over the place.' [14]

Most certainly, as Mary saw, his religion mattered for good and ill to the African; and most certainly his mind was in great confusion. But this confusion was only increased by ignorant

The 'Mind Forest'

and unsympathetic efforts by Europeans to alter him—to alter everything, including some of the most valuable of his laws and traditions. There was no consistent approach—the only agreement seemed to be that the African must be made different. To the missions, the native was 'an innocent child of nature led away and cheated by white traders and grievously oppressed by his own rulers'. To the stay-at-home statesman 'Africans are all awful savages or silly children—people who can only be dealt with on a reformatory, penitentiary line'. To many travellers he was just a curiosity. Mary believed that the white traders were on the whole his best friends, bringing him some contact with civilized standards based on the natural human transaction of trade—a relation where self-interest demanded honest dealing and a measure of common humanity and understanding. The white trader, though he often abused the Africans, usually became fond of them 'as all white men who really know Africans always do'; he 'looks after them when they are sick, or in trouble, and tries to keep them at peace with each other and with the white government, for on peace depends the prosperity which means trade'.[15]

Most other Europeans in Mary's view neither helped the Negro, nor made the best use of Africa's resources. In a letter to the negro Editor of *The New Africa* written on her voyage out to the Cape in March 1900, she described the situation as she saw it. Here are some extracts from her letter:

'The white race seems to me to blame in saying that all the reason for its interference in Africa is the improvement of the native African, and then to start on altering African institutions without in the least understanding them; and the African is to blame for not placing clearly before the Anglo-Saxon what African institutions really are. It seems to me that the leading men among the European educated Africans have depended too much on the religious side of the question. I know that

Eight Years of Achievement

there is a general opinion among the leading men of both races that Christianity will give the one possible solution to the whole problem. I fail to be able to believe this. I fail to believe Christianity will bring peace between the two races, for the simple reason that though it may be possible to convert Africans *en masse* into practical Christians it is quite impossible to convert Europeans *en masse* to it.'

Her African friend Dr Blyden answered this letter a few weeks before she died, and it seems likely she never received his reply. He stressed those features of Europeanization which were, as Mary had argued, depriving the African of his nationhood, and expressed the deepest admiration for her unique understanding of the African and his problems. He wrote:

'The Christianized negro looks away from his native heath.... He is under the curse of an insatiable ambition for imitation of foreign ideas and customs. He is afraid to turn away from the conventional conceptions of his European guides. He finds neither delight nor solace in sympathetic study of native institutions, and is therefore in no position to instruct foreigners with regard either to native law or religion. This is the black man's burden—the Christianized black man—arising not from political or social proscription, but from ignorance of the rock whence he was hewn and the hole of the pit whence he was digged—resulting in entire misapprehension of his place and work. It is hard to make the philanthropic party understand that the training they have been giving to the negro with the very best intentions is not the best for him.' [16]

It is not the business of Mary's biographer to judge how true her diagnosis of the African problem was; but rather to explain the curious fact that her travels through these jungles in which she saw so much gave her so much enjoyment. Intellectually she found these explorations exciting. In *Travels*

The 'Mind Forest'

in West Africa she says: 'Stalking the wild West African idea is one of the most charming pursuits in the world. Quite apart from the intellectual it has a high sporting interest... its pursuit is beset with difficulty and danger... And the climate in which you carry on this pursuit—vile as it is—is warm, which to me is almost an essential of existence.'

Spiritually and emotionally she found West Africa congenial. She was attracted to the unsophisticated African, and found much in his attitude to life which agreed with her own. In spite of her humble devotion to science she shared with her animistic-minded African friends a strong sense of personality in things. One could take as an example the way she describes the conduct of a ship's hawser on her first voyage which refused to remain in a place where it couldn't see life. The poetical side of her nature led her to feel intensely what Wordsworth calls the 'presences of nature'—the 'countenance' of places. A swift and deadly river seemed to her not merely a mass of mechanically impelled water, but a grand, challenging and impartial manifestation of God.

Some of her sympathy with the African's desire to propitiate irrational powers and to 'dodge' the dangers of bad-tempered spirits, may well have come from her own experiences as a child, when she had so often to manage her father's 'volcanic' outbursts, and, as she relates, to 'dodge' large objects hurled in her direction by her angry parent—whose power and personality she nevertheless admired. And she too had learnt to feel herself of little importance in the world, and had acquired in the process a deep vein of melancholy.

But between the quietist and isolationist melancholy of the Africans and her own there was a wide gulf; for they felt no responsibility for others, and she felt only too much. Her faith, though in essence Christian, lacked a Christian sense of divine protection. It was, as she told Mr Kemp, neither comfortable nor restful, since she always felt she must try to help,

Eight Years of Achievement

and was never able to believe that what went wrong was 'all for the best'.

Yet perhaps this very sense of responsibility contributed to her happiness in Africa. Here, she saw, were people she could help; a problem she could understand; an urgent job for her to do.

When she left Africa in November 1895 she was resolving and hoping to come back. But the job—of interpreting the Africans to the British—absorbed all that was left of her life.

7

The Forest of Politics

Mary Kingsley must have been conscious of her own gifts for speaking and writing, though she knew that her grammar was often shaky, and she may have known that her aspirates were often missing. She had found she could control the wild men of the bush, and she was confident that she could sway British audiences.

Both her personal appearance and her manner of speaking were a surprise to those who flocked to hear and meet her. Her broad accent and her use of slang were oddly matched with her cultured voice and natural eloquence. She had an extraordinary power of changing 'quickly and easily from jesting to a grave dignity of utterance'. She dressed, Gwynn tells us, like a superior elderly housekeeper, usually in old-fashioned black dresses and hats. Photographs bear out his description. In the one most often reproduced the face seems almost travestied by the fantastic little hat and the large satin stock and epaulettes; and we want to cover up the furbelows so as to let the nobility of her face emerge unspoiled—the powerful Kingsley features, the fine forehead, the commanding, humorous, compassionate eyes. The unpublished full-length full-face portrait which is the frontispiece to this book, adds still more incongruities. Here we see, as well as the hat and epaulettes, bracelets, rings, gloves, an umbrella, a fancy background, and tossed at the figure's feet a spray of artificial flowers. The

Eight Years of Achievement

expression of the face is very sweet; and as we look at this picture the Victorian trappings become significant and make us realize afresh the surprisingness of Mary Kingsley; for this is the woman who a year or two before, alone among wild men in the bush, was fighting her way through forest and swamp in search of knowledge and adventure.

Mary describes her own hair as hay-coloured; others called it pale gold. Her eyes were grey-blue, and her figure slim. According to Mrs St Loe Strachey she carried herself stiffly and rather resembled a ship's figure-head. The ugly clothes which appear in the photographs were fortunately not invariable. Gwynn writes of an occasion when she appeared tastefully dressed: 'I remember once a big entertainment where all sorts of literary and artistic people were assembled, and suddenly I was asked by an artist, "Who is that?" "Mary Kingsley," I answered. "But you said she was plain! She is the most beautiful person here." '

To arouse interest in West Africa, to make her audience laugh at her comments and gasp at her adventures, all this she greatly enjoyed. But her moral sense, and her ready indignation against prejudice, stupidity and humbug, soon plunged her into bitter controversy.

The first shock was administered soon after her return by an article which appeared in the *Spectator*, stimulated by the interest in West Africa she had already awakened. In the course of his article the writer referred to the Africans as a people 'abnormally low, evil, and cruel'; and suggested that they might be incapable of progress and destined to disappear. He seemed moreover to assume that she, from her experiences, agreed with him.

Mary rose in wrath. But indignation with her was apt to spread over too wide a field; and she had never accepted the cautious attitude to truth recommended by Walter Savage Landor. 'Truth', Landor said, 'in small quantities calms men;

The Forest of Politics

in greater excites them, and is capable of fatal consequences in its excess.' In her letter to the Editor in reply to this article she put all her most dangerous cards on the table; she appeared not to mind polygamy at all or cannibalism very much. She defended the drink trade and attacked the missionaries, by writing as follows:

'I do not believe the African to be brutal or degraded or cruel. I know from experience that he is often grateful and faithful and by no means the drunken idiot that his co-called friends, the Protestant missionaries, are anxious, as an excuse for their failure in dealing with him, to make out.' [1]

This outburst might have had fatal consequences to Mary as a champion of West Africa: that it did not was due to several causes. Among these were her growing popularity with the general public; and the obvious extent of her first-hand knowledge. And the fact that she was from this very first article taking up the cause of the traders, won her the approval and support of leading merchants in Liverpool and Manchester. Her later articles were more diplomatic, and the propaganda contained in her lectures was usually tactful and persuasive.

When she returned from Africa she was not prepared for the complexity and tangled strands of government policies and theories. Here was a forest in which she found it very difficult to 'see'. Like most women who have turned to politics from disinterested desire to further a just cause, she began by believing that knowledge of facts reasonably presented and ethical principles could be made the determining factors of policy. She was rapidly disillusioned, and in the process became sometimes unjustly bitter and suspicious. There were not many public men whom she wholly trusted, though there came to be many who trusted her.

One of her firmest and most unvarying friendships was for the merchant John Holt of Liverpool. As we have seen, Mary

Eight Years of Achievement

liked the world of commerce. Perhaps it was a sign of fellow-feeling with business men which led to her remark to Sir Alfred Lyall, 'I have always felt that our business men, if they had been left to themselves to make a religion, would have turned out something uncommonly like Juju.' There were many things in John Holt which appealed strongly to Mary. He had built up a great enterprise through individual effort, and had spent many years in West Africa as a young man in conditions of loneliness and danger. He was a man of great personal integrity; a man she entirely trusted and one of the few she came to think 'wise enough and kind enough to manage West Africa'. When the controversy about the justice of imposing a hut tax in British West Africa was at its height, Mary exchanged a vast number of letters with Holt. He could and did provide her with a mass of information, both about trade conditions on the Coast and details of his own business. She on her side, according to an obituary notice of Holt contributed by Mrs Green to the African Society in 1915, stimulated him to 'reflect on the larger issues of his business' and to 'gather his isolated experiences into a coherent body of thought. That correspondence, if it could be recovered, would be of priceless value.'[2] His letters unfortunately do not seem to have survived; hers, preserved and cherished by the present firm of John Holt & Company, give a most vivid picture of her struggles in defence of the Africans, and her own hopes, fears, opinions, dejections, angers and unceasing efforts. She poured out her heart to him—her political heart, which in her was never very far, as she often reveals, from her emotional one. Between November 1897 and the spring of 1900 she wrote to him every few days.

The ins and outs of British policy in West Africa during the last half of the nineteenth century are matters for the historian; Mary's biographer is concerned with the view of these complexities which presented itself to her. She was frankly an

The Forest of Politics

imperialist, and she believed we had a perfect right to exploit for our own use the vast riches of West Africa which the inhabitants had shown themselves incapable of developing, and to prevent these from being seized by our competitors, provided that in so doing we improved the conditions of life for the African population and respected the best elements in their laws and customs. The exploitation must be carried on with reasonable humanity, and with strict regard for 'honour'—for the keeping of promises made even to the most uncivilized tribes. On this subject of British honour she constantly harped; and she believed that more honesty and humanity were shown by the traders than by the armchair pundits of the Colonial Office whose knowledge of West Africa was so largely confined to the Coast, and who never themselves went near the pestilent place.

What mainly provoked her into a vehement defence of the traders was her conviction that a philanthropic façade was being given by the Government to inefficient administration by an attack on the liquor traffic; an attack which enlisted the support of the mission and temperance bodies and represented the traders as men who, regardless of the welfare of Africans, forced liquor—and often adulterated liquor at that—on ignorant and helpless Negroes. Mary's fear and hatred of humbug led her to be sometimes unfairly suspicious of the 'philanthropic' party, including the mission party in Exeter House. But she had some good grounds for suspicion. She mentions in an early letter to Mr Holt that—'an English politician said to me the other day "you see, if we attack the sale of liquor in England to the extent the temperance party wish, we should alienate from our party a great mass of votes, but when attacking the sale of liquor to native races we hurt nobody" '.[3]

She seems to have taken a too lenient view of the harm done in West Africa by imports of liquor. Drunkenness was probably worse on the coast, where she had travelled less widely

Eight Years of Achievement

than in the hinterland. But she knew that the Africans brewed far more harmful forms of alcohol for themselves; and that the foul water they often drank was more dangerous than British rum. An extract from her diary given in *Travels in West Africa* reports:

'On my way back I notice the people getting water from the stinking streams; small wonder the mortality is high in Libreville: this is usually attributed to the inhabitants "going it", but they might "go it" more than they do without killing themselves if they left off drinking this essence of stinking slime.' [4]

She was convinced that reputable British firms and their agents, many of whom had become her personal friends, were incapable of adulterating the liquor they sold, and she confirmed this view by submitting a number of samples for analysis.

It incensed Mary to find the men whom she regarded as serving the interests of Britain under most difficult conditions, being ignored, or used as scape-goats by the Government. She argued that merchants and shipowners, like Holt and A. L. Jones of Liverpool, with their extensive knowledge of the Coast, should, so far from being cold-shouldered by the Government, be consulted on many matters of West African policy, and given definite advisory status; and that colonial trade interests should have special representation in Parliament.

For some years she fought hard to persuade the Government and the merchants themselves to set up a council of traders of this kind. In the end she failed, partly because of the difficulties the merchants had in making common cause, and partly because of a snobbish attitude towards trade on the part of officials.

Her criticism of missions, her tolerance of the liquor traffic, her passionate defence of traders, laid her open to attacks from many sides. She was accused of being paid by Liverpool to advocate policies favourable to their commercial interests, and

The Forest of Politics

even of prostituting her science to that end. She was referred to in some quarters, she tells Holt, as 'Liverpool's hired assassin'. In December 1897 she writes to him: 'What I have said to offend the C.O. is what I have said about the liquor trade—the prohibition of liquors is their strong point. . . . I am regarded, I am told, as the last trump in the hands of the liquor party. Nice situation for a lady icthyologist!' [5]

But the battle of the traders was only one of the contests into which Mary threw herself in these last years. Two years after her return she was involved in the battle of the Hut Tax.

The Hut Tax was imposed in order to raise funds for policing and developing the large territories lying inland from the British colony of Sierra Leone. It was a form of tax which the Africans intensely resented; and an earlier attempt to impose such a tax had aroused so much resistance that it had been withdrawn. This new proposal was greeted by protests and petitions from the chiefs who would have to collect the tax; but the chiefs were brutally handled and their objections disregarded. A widespread revolt led to much bloodshed among both Africans and British; but little was said about all this in the British press. Mary entered the lists with a strong article in the *Spectator* in March 1898. In it she wrote: 'The recurring attempt to levy hut-tax and its recurring rows are common to all Africa for exactly the same reason, namely, that this form of taxation is abhorrent to the principles of African law. One of the root principles of African law is that the thing you pay anyone a regular fee for is a thing that is not your own. . . . The African understands and accepts taxes on trade, but taxing a man's individual possession is a violation of his idea of property.' It must be remembered that we had not conquered the lands we were administering, but had acquired, by agreement with chiefs, only certain supervisory powers. The Hut Tax was regarded by many Africans as a first step to depriving them of their country.

Eight Years of Achievement

Knowing that John Holt was opposed to the Hut Tax, both from commercial interest in peaceful conditions on the Coast and from his own knowledge of the Africans, Mary persuaded him to follow up her article by a letter. The Chambers of Commerce of Liverpool and Manchester had already protested against the tax in vain, since it was not the custom of the Government, as Mary had already pointed out, to learn from the traders about conditions in the hinterland. Her article helped to consolidate opposition to the tax, and within two months the matter had been discussed in Parliament and a Commission of Inquiry had been appointed.

Joseph Chamberlain was at this time at the head of the Colonial Office, and it is an extraordinary testimony to Mary's influence that already in March 1897 she had been invited to talks with him. By April she was in constant communication with him. She tells Mr Holt, in strict confidence, that: 'Chamberlain is manifesting a desire to be taught. He is horribly frightened of being known to communicate with me, à la Saul and the witch of Endor. . . . I am secretly inserting into him on a dozen sides the horror of the thing he has done with this hut tax and he turns to me asking if I can give him any suggestions as to an alternative method of collecting revenue.' [6] 'Now once a week', she wrote to Mr Kemp on 25 April, 'I get a letter from him, and he gets a massive answer. . . . He doesn't stick to his hut-tax only now, but asks suggestions on all sorts of points, and I am let in for writing a general and particular scheme for the administration of West Africa.' [7]

A third battle in which Mary would have become more involved if she had had the necessary authority, was the battle of concessions. She was distressed to see territories which she believed to be very important for British trade and influence in Africa being encircled, or bargained away for doubtful diplomatic advantages with other countries, notably France, who was then our chief rival in West Africa.

Mary Kingsley, in 1896 or 1897

The Forest of Politics

On the subject of a right-minded imperialism she had much to say in her public lectures.

Her belief in British Imperialism was profound, but her conception of what it should involve led her to oppose equally any patronizing or bullying of the Africans and any rash idealism which would encourage them to seek self-determination long before they were ready for it. At the close of a lecture given in Oxford in 1897 she said:

'Of the great importance of the study of the religion, laws and social status of the African native it is not necessary for me to speak; it is self-evident that it is our duty to know the true nature of those people with whom we are now dealing in tens of thousands, so that by this knowledge we may be enabled to rule them wisely, to give them chances of advancing which they can really avail themselves of, and thereby save thousands of human lives, both black and white, by means of that true knowledge I regard as the inward aid of God.'

Of course she knew very well that this conception of our duty to Africans was far from 'self-evident' to most of the men engaged in governing them, and early and late, in writings, articles and speeches, she repeated her plea 'get understanding', and quoted her favourite passage from Spinoza about the inward aid of God.

She was found to be an expert among experts on a surprising number of subjects, and was consulted not only about methods of government in Africa, but also on economic and currency problems. And not only by British authorities but by those of several other countries. Her knowledge of the French Congo led to constant communications with French diplomats, who sought her advice about their uneconomic administration and tariffs. John Holt was able to give her additional information on these subjects. For example, on 24 December 1898 she wrote to him:

Eight Years of Achievement

'I copied out word for word your statement on the Metropolitan Tariff, and de Manville* has communicated the gist of it to his government and to his party, the Colonial. They seem born idiots on commerce, and they evidently have but little knowledge of how their colonies are governed; they seem to feel it profoundly sad that their colonies don't pay, just as our people cannot make out how with all the advantages of civilization afforded them they don't civilize.'

Again a few weeks later she reports that the French Embassy have been groaning to her about the horrible expense of their colonies, and adds: 'I will tell them why without implicating the English traders.' And in the following July she writes:

'Vicomte de Manville has been in this afternoon, and is highly diverted at the pleasure the C.O. has shown over me; he thinks if France wants an investigator of her colonies the C.O. will throw no obstacle in her way of securing me; he also says I am said to have stirred up a revolution in Liverpool and Manchester. That's all the thanks I get from a grateful country!'⁸

Mary was the acknowledged leader of educated Africans, and formed a close friendship with the distinguished negro scholar, Dr Edward Blyden. She was in constant touch with colonial administrators and governors, including Lord Lugard. She does not seem to have recognized how much Lugard's attitude to African problems agreed with her own; but it was not till long after her death that he was able to give effect to these ideals. She discussed suitable coinage systems for West Africa with the banker Sir Samuel Montagu, and became a friend of his and of his wife. Indeed most of her contacts, whether accompanied by agreements or disagreements, seem to have ripened into friendships. Even of Sir Frederick Cardew, the instigator of the Sierra Leone Hut Tax, she wrote to a friend:

* Vicomte de Manneville (Mary was given to misspelling people's names) was at the time secretary to the French Embassy in London.

The Forest of Politics

'Still, I like Sir Frederick Cardew. It is my melancholy fate to like so many people I profoundly disagree with and to often heartily dislike people who agree with me.' [9] One of her most intimate associations was with Sir George Goldie and his family. She had an immense admiration for Goldie's character and for the work he had done as head of the Royal Niger Company, and wrote about him in glowing terms in her *Story of West Africa*. But she had many and violent arguments with him, and she had difficulty in combating the distrust which existed between Goldie and Holt, representing as they did rival interests of a chartered company with its attendant privileges and an independent trader.

Much of the information she was able to give had a practical bearing on such things as the making of roads and railways. She knew where the inland trade routes ran through the bush, and what districts were the most dangerous to the health of both white and black workers. She was always insisting that while the death rate for Europeans in Africa remained so terribly high, only very carefully planned and very necessary developments should be undertaken, and only those which the Africans themselves could be persuaded to approve of and work at with goodwill under British supervision.

Through the progress of science in which she so ardently believed, the dangers from disease in West Africa have been very much lessened, and it is no longer a 'white man's grave'. But the dangers of making ecological and cultural blunders persist. One feels that if Mary Kingsley had been here to give advice—and to be listened to—the mistakes of starting in unsuitable conditions a groundnut scheme or poultry ranches would have been avoided. She could have foretold, for example, that local labourers would be unwilling to clear away their favourite ju-ju trees for the establishing of a chicken ranch.

She would have foreseen the trouble caused in Africa by constant pilfering—a weakness about which she is very

Eight Years of Achievement

amusing in her books, but which can be very serious to such a man as Dr Schweitzer in his hospital. Describing the troubles of the British trader, Mary points out how thieving was far more easily checked by a belief in Fetish than by any number of policemen and prisons. After all the policeman is often absent or asleep, but the fetish spirit whose material habitation is suspended in a tree to guard someone's property, is omnipresent and all-seeing. It is obvious that the European trader whose goods were not protected by a charm which would cause any thief to swell up and burst, was comparatively easy prey.

Mary understood and constantly pointed out that many of the difficulties which face the European in Africa are due to misguided attempts at Westernization which have resulted in a 'disintegration of native culture'. She writes at length in *West African Studies* of the graft and injustice often practised by one black man against another when the white man's newly created protégé, the African clerk or soldier, free from the control of his own tribe and chief and his own fetish prohibitions, uses his privileges to wreak his private vengeances and to defraud his fellows.

Though Mary's anthropological knowledge was her strongest weapon in any controversy, the extent to which she was armed with a wide knowledge of facts relating to the history of colonialism, of trade past and present, of the geography, climate and prevalent diseases of West Africa, made her a formidable adversary. As Morel wrote after her death, in the *British Empire Review*: 'The changes she advocated were so drastic that many regarded her as a visionary. Never was visionary better supplied with facts to substantiate a vision.' She was always ready to back up her arguments with statistics. Statistics, she said, were music to her. As a woman she was shy and self-effacing, as a scientist and reformer she was pugnacious and bold. It was bound to cause resentment among some of those whose information and opinions she questioned, that a

The Forest of Politics

young woman unknown a few years previously, and lacking the status of wealth or powerful family connexions, should keep bobbing up over political affairs, and in lectures and articles demonstrating the unwisdom and ignorance of officialdom.

She was represented by some of her opponents as 'dangerous', 'insidious' and an 'unscrupulous politician'. The fighting Kingsley side of her enjoyed the fray. 'Personally I do not care', she wrote to Mr Holt, at the height of the Hut Tax controversy, 'how much Chamberlain and C.O. hate me so long as they fear me.' [10] A year previously she had told Mr Holt that chapters of her book, *West African Studies*, dealing with the Crown Colony system, would be 'a perfect hornpipe on the corns of the Colonial Office'.

But the harshness and irony, like the joy of battle, were only superficial. Most of those who knew her or listened to her were more aware of the humanity than of the mockery. 'I have just come from a function', she tells Mr Holt, 'with a bouquet swarming with insects, and the statement of the Revd Prebendary Wilkinson that "that sweet pathos which Miss K combines with a radiant humour" etc etc.' [11] Sir George Goldie had accused her of being influenced by 'pure sentiment', a remark which she resented; you might just as well, she declared, call science or commerce sentiment. Nevertheless it was true that she cared about the future of the Africans and of the lonely West Coast British traders, cared, as she implies in another letter to Holt, in the way that some men care for their wives; this love for Africa was her romance. And it was bitter, when the political battle seemed a losing one, to be kept away from travel and exploration by apparently futile diplomatic talk and paper warfare.

Disappointments were many. Even her plans for a West African newspaper, and for a society of African anthropologists, were not realized during her lifetime. A sense of failure brought her frequent moods of 'sackcloth and ashes'. In these moods

Eight Years of Achievement

Holt was one of her main comforters—for he believed in her, and told her so, and he understood her problems. In March 1899 she wrote to him: 'I can never adequately express my obligations to you, and not least among them is being allowed to speak out to you without any ulterior motive, without playing any game. I feel as if I were always playing games up here with these people, it amuses me, but underneath I hate it, but I must do it for the stakes are men's lives.' [12]

She certainly enlightened the general public and the Colonial Office about many features of West African life; and though she did not succeed in getting the Hut Tax removed, or in persuading the Colonial Office to consult more freely with the merchants, it is a fact that subsequent taxation was imposed with more circumspection and understanding.

The Hut Tax had been instituted by the Governor of Freetown, Sir Frederick Cardew, a man whose insight into the minds of the Africans amongst whom he had lived Mary compared to that of a British Museum policeman into the cuneiform inscriptions he sees every day. When, largely as a result of her protests, a Special Commission was sent out to report on the tax, the Commissioner, Sir David Chalmers, confirmed most of her contentions, but the Government postponed the publication of his Report from month to month and pushed on with the tax.

In August 1898 Sir David Chalmers died, before his report had seen the light. Mary wrote to John Holt:

'I enclose you a letter from Lady Chalmers, is it not *terrible*! I saw her brother last night and he told me Sir David grieved and grieved over the suppression of his report, he felt the horrors of the thing going on, and he could not think why the British Government should be so quiet and taking no action to stop it. It is clear this worry went more to killing him than residence in Sierra Leone. I do hope you great merchant adven-

The Forest of Politics

turers of England will never forget Chalmers, and will gradually realize that you as Englishmen *must* pull yourselves together and become a fighting force and a governing force in a region with which your honour is so closely connected as well as your profit. I have no faith in any other party.'

In the same letter, which was obviously written under great stress of feeling, she says of Chalmers that he was a trained experienced lawyer who without any influence from her had produced a report which bore out her ethnological arguments to the hilt; and had at the same time given 'an account of atrocities which if they had been reported in the territory of a foreign power would have flamed up popular opinion here to fury'.[13]

At first Mary had had hopes of Chamberlain; she ended by having little faith in the whole machinery of government, and this disillusionment may have some bearing on her opposition to women's suffrage. Her attitude on this question was partly due no doubt to the fact that, though she had a great respect for the work done by women in their homes, she was mainly interested in a masculine world of enterprise and adventure. And experience had led her to believe that the most important work for humanity was done *outside* Parliament. She tells Mr Holt in July 1899 that she has taken part in a discussion on women's suffrage and has argued against it. He seems to have reproved her for her attitude, for a few days later she writes:

'Thank you for what you say about the ladies. I really think I help them more than some of those shrieking females and androgins with whom they are so mixed up. The worst of it is, you see, women are very like business men, the majority of the most representative of them have not got the time to give to public affairs; how could Mrs Holt go into parliament with

Eight Years of Achievement

comfort to herself. Flora Shaw* and I could, but we should not be as good as Mrs Holt. Still on the whole women are in the mass more honest in purpose and more unselfish, and they are not an atom more fickle than men. I do not think if they had votes it would make much difference in the end for bad or good, it would only make our political machinery more cumbersome.' [14]

The manuscript notes of a speech she delivered at a Conference on Women's Suffrage have been preserved.[15] It was in her usual lively, vivid, comic and serious style, and in the course of it she made very plain how disillusioned she had become with the machinery of government. She believed that what was needed was far more expert knowledge among M.P.s and more information and responsible thought among electors. She felt the addition of a mass of even less well-informed women would only make matters worse. And she argued that just because women were often more independent in their judgements than men were, they would be unwilling to 'sacrifice conviction to party . . . or combine against a common foe on a party emotion. They are therefore unfit for parliament and parliament is unfit for them.'

She urged that women should instead take an increasingly active part in local government, while exercising the right of free and independent critics on other aspects of political life *from outside*. She herself, she once told Holt, preferred working 'through a man', as it left her 'a free hand to fight with'.

But how free is such a hand? Mary seems to have been overlooking the great difficulty women have always found in putting their criticisms across *from outside*. And the inconsistency of her attitude is surprising since she was well aware of what she called in one article 'the morbid state of opinion regarding

---

* Flora Shaw—afterwards Lady Lugard—was a prominent contributor to *The Times* on West African affairs.

The Forest of Politics

women's work', and her own efforts had been hampered by the fact that at that time women were so little accepted—or expected—as critics of the government of their country. After urging that women should take more part in scientific and artistic work where there are no sex barriers, she concluded her speech by saying that she had received generous and impartial recognition for her scientific work, but she added: 'I have failed *miserably*, more miserably than I can say, to get recognition for the most practically important part of it'—and she was alluding to the political part.

On the occasions when Mary felt that her efforts to help West Africa were wasted, she was naturally 'sick at heart'; for she devoted four strenuous years to this cause. The amount of work she got through is astounding. In those four years she had produced her two long books, one of them, *West African Studies*, including six chapters which were in effect a reply to Chamberlain's request for criticism and advice on the administration of Crown Colonies. She also wrote a short book intended to interest working men—*The Story of West Africa*. She was constantly asked for articles on questions relating to Africa, and sometimes wrote them in answer to a telegram in the small hours of the night. As a lecturer she was in demand by scientific bodies and by what were then called 'philosophical' societies up and down the country. She gave lectures to schools, and many unpaid lectures in aid of charities; she even lectured for missions, mostly it seems for the Nonconformists for whose work in Africa she had more respect than for that of the Anglicans, and among whom was her friend Mr Kemp. But the atmosphere of chapels disconcerted her. She wrote to George Macmillan:

'I should dearly like to take photographs of some of my audiences—and chairmen. At that Highbury quadrant I had 1700 people. I addressed them from a red-velvet lined pulpit,

Eight Years of Achievement

surrounded by the ministers and elders. Three times last week I spoke in miscellaneous chapels and had tea with the deacons, grim old budgeroons.'

From a breathless letter to John Holt one can get an idea of the *tempo* of some of those lecture tours and of the humorous way in which she regarded them.

Nov. 29, 1899. 'I have had no time or been too tired to write a line since last Friday week when I left London for York; at York I gave a lecture in aid of the Y.P.S. (?York Philosophical Society) which is devoted to Roman Remains and £3000 in debt, an awful warning which I hope you will remember should you feel a passionate desire to take up archaeology, which is plainly a dangerous thing to mix oneself up in, for the President as a reward to me took me round the walls of York Saturday and showed me all the Roman remains in York, in a bitter kind of blizzard, meaning well but nearly killing me. Saturday evening I made Newcastle in spite of bad weather. Sunday I lectured to two thousand people in a theatre, draughty, on W.A. Monday ditto to N.P.S. Tuesday to Edinburgh and lectured on W.A. to high toned Scotch audience, successfully. Wednesday partially recovered. Thursday Glasgow, awful goings on, bonfire with magic lantern. Friday Dundee, 1800—great enthusiasm. Saturday reached Edinburgh again for repairs, tomorrow Monday Aberdeen, Tuesday Glasgow again, Wednesday Hawick the L. and Y. Railway Depot, Friday Birmingham, Saturday home, and a thorough careening and breaming and new tackle, and then Halifax, and Birmingham again—I will not dwell on the painful subject further.' [16]

The painful subject—and its painfulness was often real enough as she was frequently ill during these years, with influenza, headaches and heart trouble—seems invariably to have been presented to her friends as a subject for laughter. To Mrs Green she wrote of one of her tours:

The Forest of Politics

'Lordy! The times I have had this past week—awful adventures at Leicester—champion of the liquor traffic had to sleep at a temperance hotel in a wine cupboard because of horse-races. Sheffield also weird. I realized at Leeds that I did not know where I was to lecture at Sheffield, so telegraphed to ask. They answered "literary-philosophical" so I thought it was there. Well, when I went there ten minutes before the time—it wasn't. Building deserted; frantic rush into chemist's shop to ask where the philosophical was holding its meeting—gay young chemist says, "Oh I can't tell you, I know they've got a big pot down for the Phil, and they've hired a special hall." Briefly mentioning I was the big pot, I left him and toiled into a stationer's—young woman at stationer's knew and would take me there. Saved!!! Off we went at full speed; landed at hall placarded "Escaped Nun and Father Slattery"; hissed by crowd for escaped nun—fled back to philosophical society, outside which were two gentlemen evidently devoid of philosophy, and they told me they were the secretaries, who had lost their lecturer and had 1400 people getting savage round the corner in an old Music Hall.' [17]

In addition to lecturing and writing she had a very full social life. She regarded the running of her home and keeping it comfortable for her brother as a duty—'the religion I was brought up in'. She entertained and was entertained on a large scale. Friends of many nationalities braved the poisoned arrows and evil-looking and evil-smelling ju-ju objects which decorated her home, first at 100 Addison Road, and later at St Mary Abbot's Terrace, Hammersmith. Men in high official positions came there seeking her advice. She was invited to political dinners and country house week-ends, where she met many distinguished people. Among these was Lord Cromer, whom she met at the St Loe Stracheys, and who said to his hosts the next day that 'he had never met a woman who impressed him

Eight Years of Achievement

so much as having the mind of a statesman'. Her circle of acquaintances was vast, and her friends many. Yet with all this she still found time for her true love, science. She writes to Holt:

'I do think it rather hard I cannot go out of sight around corners amusing myself without being suspected of dire and awful crimes against the British Constitution, however such is the case with all my friends. If I do not turn up regularly at the Anthropological the Anthropological suspects me of balls and parties, if I do stick to the Anthropological, other sections suspect me. You should just hear Dr Günther at present because I have not been over there helping him with decayed fish. I *did* go over only the other day and worked for hours, and stank so that people noticed a "strange smell" at luncheon and dinner parties I was present at for a week after. It is a cruel world.' [18]

She corresponded at length with other workers in her own field and did much to help and encourage the less well known— among them her friend Mr Dennett. But the practical side of every question was always intruding on her conscience and forcing her back into politics. To one of her anthropological friends, Mr Hartland, she wrote:

'I have been fighting with my back against the wall ever since I came home for the employment of anthropological knowledge in the government of tropical Africa. Tylor told me it was worth fighting for and I felt so too from what I saw of things, and the other day Lord Cromer when he was over here sent for me and expressed his opinion of the value of it—but do those clerks listen! No!!' (By the clerks she means the Colonial Office.) 'Of course I do not talk to the uninitiated like this. I say: "see what a lot of money you will save if you will only be good and learn your lessons etc." ... And I have hopes of them yet.... What really stands in the way of the introduction of anthropology into statecraft is Exeter Hall and the Aborigines Protection Society. They have quite spoilt the

The Forest of Politics

temper of the people up here and they think any concession to native ideas shows weakness and involves a loss of prestige, while even the mission party shy at science.' [19]

The *Manchester Guardian*, then at the height of its influence under C. P. Scott, declared that *West African Studies* contained the most damaging attack on the general administration of West Africa that had yet been made. 'Miss Kingsley has followed no school of West African policy, but, if we mistake not, she has laid the foundation of one.' Equally the Tory paper, the *St James Gazette*, took the line that 'it will be impossible for the Colonial Office to disregard the warning given'.[20]

At the end of *The Story of West Africa* she wrote with appreciation of Chamberlain's interest in the development of West Africa and of efforts which were being made to apply science to its many problems—both medical science and anthropology. Only when this was done on a large scale, she thought, could we hope to civilize Africa—'cease to kill unnecessarily . . . and cease to spoil as we now do, a very fine race of human beings at considerable expense and to no one's profit. . . . Not by mere human drifting, striving, narrow effort, nor by emotionalism, however pure, can we succeed in West Africa. With "the inward aid of God", as Spinoza calls Science, we can.'

Mary Kingsley did not live long enough to see either the successes or the failures in applying the policies she advocated; both are very visible to us fifty years after her death.

Though she may have seen little practical result from her work it is clear that she knew she had power over the minds of men, and that she was using it to bring about a more enlightened attitude to subject races at a time when Britain was suffering from an overdose of narrow self-satisfaction and arrogance. The *Westminster Gazette* reviewing *West African Studies* wrote that the secret of Miss Kingsley's remarkable influence was that she 'expressed everything in terms of humanity'.

8

Books and Friends

In the way she wrote her books Mary Kingsley was as original as in everything else she did; constantly alternating between precision and impulse. If we are to get the fullest enjoyment and instruction from her travel books we must be ready to accept their mixture of ingredients as given, and above all to tolerate their discursiveness and length.

The period to which Mary belonged was distinguished by an attitude to 'The Truth' amounting to idolatry. It was the period in which Clough had declared that it fortified his soul to know that though he perished Truth *'was so'*. Mary shared to the full the Victorian scientists' respect for The Truth; but she could not find the eternal 'Is so' as comforting as Clough affected to do; and she often found it both sad and funny. The flavour of her writing lies in its peculiar mixture of earnest research and hilarious comment; of recognition of a stern divine law, and pity for man's difficulties in adjusting to it.

Her books are long and thronged with detail because she wanted to build up an objective picture; but this picture was intended to stimulate judgement and sympathy in her readers. In the preface to *West African Studies* she says of her chapters on systems of government in Africa:

'I cannot show you anything clearly and neatly. I have to show you a series of pictures of things and hope you will get

Books and Friends

from those pictures the impression which is the truth. I dare not set myself up to tell you the truth. I only say, look at it; and to the best of my ability faithfully give you, not an artist's picture, but a photograph, an over-laden with detail, colourless version; all the time wishing to Heaven there was someone else doing it who could do it better, and then I know you would understand, and all would be well. I know there are people who tax me with a brutality in statement, I feel unjustly; and it makes me wonder what they would say if they had to speak about West Africa.'

'I cannot get outside the seething mass of things', she wrote to Macmillan when preparing *West African Studies* for the press; 'I am holding on to the main idea, round which it is written, by the scruff of its neck, but the selection of the facts which will bring that idea clearly out to the minds of people who do not know is hard work. . . . If I did not know so much, it would be easier.'

To St Loe Strachey soon after the publication of the book she wrote: 'My opinion on my style is fixed, but I do not wish everyone to share it. The only thing that worries me is that it is not sufficiently clear. My only way of approaching clearness of expression or description is *via* diffuseness.' [1]

Part of the diffuseness and repetition was also due to her need to establish herself, by sheer mass of evidence, as one with a right to speak. Owing to that 'morbid state of opinion regarding women's work' to which she referred, the time she said was 'unpleasant for any student who happens to be a woman to come before the public'. In any case a traveller in the wildest regions of West Africa needed to be careful of his reputation for veracity.

Another thing which added to the length of her books and which arose from her scrupulous regard for accuracy, was her

Eight Years of Achievement

habit of carefully docketing the information she acquired from other writers and travellers. It appears that she had studied West Africa for some fifteen years before she went there, hence the background of knowledge which provided the fascinating Appendices to her two volumes, treating of ancient voyagers, Colonial history, and trade and labour conditions.

Travels in West Africa is further enlarged by a series of notes by Dr Günther on the unknown or rare species of insects and fishes which Mary had brought back. Three species of fish were called after her: and one cannot doubt that the large plate representing *Ctenopoma Kinsleyae* was a page of the book she would not have wished to omit.

Obviously the mass of facts, so many of them unknown or unappreciated, which she wanted to convey, and the reforms she wanted to advocate, involved a long book. Added to them there was her own dramatic feeling for the comic human episode. She could not bring herself to leave out many queer and entertaining revelations of the oddity and variety of human nature.

Both the subject-matter and the style of Mary's books led to controversy with her friends. She was made timid by knowing how entirely self-educated she was. When she was writing *West African Studies* she thought it wise to reassure her publisher by telling him that her friend Miss Toulmin-Smith was reading over her proofs: 'She is an acknowledged authority on grammar, and I am struck by the way she tolerates mine. She says it is *very good sixteenth century* on the whole.' It was largely, as we know, from tales of the early buccaneers that the youthful Mary had acquired her knowledge of English.

Because she was diffident she consulted her friends about her books; but because she was a Kingsley, and had at all costs to be herself, she rejected most of their counsel.

Travels in West Africa needed a map—but she had explored some little-known and some uncharted country and no accept-

John Holt, *c.* 1900

Books and Friends

able map could be found.* Mary refused a make-shift map. She wrote to Macmillan:

'I have got the name in Liverpool and on the Coast of knowing more about the geography of the West Coast as a whole than anyone, and for me to issue a sketchy skeleton that would not pass muster at a missionary meeting—well, I'd rather be excused.'

Then Dr Guillemard's re-writing of some of her diary included in the *Travels* had resulted in a paragraph which gave a quite wrong view of the depth of water in Forçados Bar—as well as having introduced expressions wholly un-nautical. She wrote to Macmillan:

'I see quite clearly that I cannot publish this sort of thing. . . . I am going down the Coast again and I have no character to lose as a literary person, but I have got a very good character to lose as a practical seaman and an honest observer of facts on the West Coast. . . . I have taken vessels of 2000 tons across that Bar as a pilot three times. I should never get the chance of taking another if I published such rot, and I would rather take a 200 ton vessel up a creek than write any book.'

Then there was that 'brutality in statement' to which she refers in her preface to *West African Studies*; over that she had many battles. One of these she lost, temporarily. The brilliant and entertaining chapter describing the characters and conversation of seamen and traders on her first voyage, was omitted from the *Travels*. It reappears quite out of place as Chapter I of *West African Studies*. By then she had become a popular writer; her first book had sold well and fast and she could have her own way over what, and how, she wrote.

* It is still hard to find a clear map of the regions she explored. For the Ogowé River the French Surveys are the best, but they confine themselves mainly to trade routes.

Eight Years of Achievement

This chapter contains awful warnings and grim descriptions of the many different kinds of death which await the traveller in West Africa, as retailed by the old Coasters. Most of these stories Mary asserts to be true. But there are, she admits, a few tales so tall that one may be excused from believing them, especially since 'in these days it is the duty of everyone to keep their beliefs for religious purposes'. Sly ironies of this kind in her books, and unsavoury details, aroused anxiety among her friends and advisers. She wrote to Macmillan that her friend Mrs Green was 'horrified' at this chapter.

'She always tells me, just as Guillemard did, that I *ought not* to go on like that. Take myself seriously, etc. I really *am* always serious and "duller than a great Thaw" compared with the things I speak of, and I feel you cannot understand W.A. unless you understand the steamboat. Moreover, I do not want to be *anyone*, and this laughable stuff is in the thing just as the Fetish etc. is; and when Lyall and Mrs G. and Guillemard and so on come along and expect me to stand on my head, all my innate vulgarity breaks out.'

She tried to be accommodating where she could. To Lady Macdonald she wrote: 'The amount of expurgation my journals have required has been awful. My well-known veneration for Governors, Consul-Generals and Bishops has necessitated much crossing out.' And to George Macmillan: 'I am rigorously cutting out all the poetry and bad language, except the native legal oaths.' There is a subtle suggestion that poetry and bad language had some affinities in her mind; certainly liberty and poetry had; consequently she could little endure interference with her style. Moreover, when she chose she could adapt her style to her aims; *The Story of West Africa* written to appeal to working men is lucid and straightforward and without the quips and ironies which characterize her longer books.

Books and Friends

To a Cambridge friend she wrote after the publication of her first book:

'It's a little hard of you to say it is wonderful of me to "keep it up" right through that book of mine. Of course I could not "keep it up", that was the reason why I could not accept Dr G's editing. Fancy having to do those seven hundred pages on stilts! and those 700 only give a thumb-nail sketch of what I know of W.A.' [2]

Between Mary and Dr Guillemard a squall had blown up over this question of her style. He had kindly undertaken to read over the *Travels* before publication to check certain scientific statements; but he went so far as to re-write and to alter Mary's mode of expression. She was conscious of its faults but, a poor thing or not, it was her own, and she was not prepared to accept more than occasional advice. In her Preface to *West African Studies* she says:

'I am not a literary man, only a student of West Africa. I am not proud of my imperfections in English. I would write better if I could, but I cannot. I find when I try to write like other people that I do not say what seems to me true, and thereby lose all right to say anything.'

But in fact she *was* a literary man. Large portions of her books by their range and originality of vocabulary, sense of rhythm and phrasing, allusiveness and wit, power of vivid evocation, have every claim to rank as literature. Their chief fault, and it is one found in many more famous books, is their unevenness, and this has tended to overshadow the finer qualities.

The great British public did not hesitate—these long, factual, comical, disordered books were enthusiastically bought and read. 'I am popular', Mary wrote to Mr Kemp when advising him about some writing of his own, 'because I am natural.'

Eight Years of Achievement

As for the poetry—the kind of poetry she averred she had cut out along with the bad language—fortunately she left in pages and pages of that in the form of vivid and exquisitely phrased descriptions of strange places and events, many of which have been quoted in earlier chapters of this biography. Whether she ever wrote poetry proper is uncertain. Stephen Gwynn quotes two contradictory statements of hers on the subject; in one she wrote to him that she wished she could write poetry, but it was not in her and she had never written any. He then quotes from a letter to George Macmillan saying:

'This London life takes all the go out of me. I have not written a poem for months, which is an awful bad symptom for me. All those bits the papers say are pretty are of rough rhyme stuff with some of the rhyme knocked out afterwards.'

No serious student of literature will accept this last statement —fine prose like much of Mary's was never made from poetry with the rhymes knocked out. If she did write any actual poetry it has perished, by her own hand or by those of her curiously careless relatives, along with those invaluable diaries.

On receiving her first cheque she wrote to thank Macmillan for having risked publication.

'You knew the public better than I. I thought they really cared for nothing but art and geographical facts, though I have had a sneaking feeling that there must be some people who care for things as they are, with all the go and glory and beauty in them as well as the mechanism and the microbes.'

In spite of the naturalness and often almost childlike directness of her manner of writing and speaking, Mary Kingsley remained an enigma to most of her contemporaries. The crowds at her lectures who saw her standing stiffly and shyly before them to receive their applause never suspected that, while genuinely grateful for their tributes, she was amusing herself

Books and Friends

by noticing the grim old budgeroons in her audience and the insects on her bouquet. Her friends on the other hand often failed to recognize the sadness and intellectual unrest that lay beneath her gaiety and fun.

The picture of her which has emerged from these last pages may suggest that she must have been a tiring sort of person to know—so much controversy and argument; such torrents of correspondence; so much propaganda; so many brickbats and stilettos flying about. But in fact her acquaintances welcomed her as a delightful companion, and those who knew her well found her a source of both comfort and inspiration, and infinitely kind. 'Quite the most amusing person I ever met' said Mrs St Loe Strachey. E. D. Morel, with whom she was intimate, wrote in 1902 a Foreword to his book *Affairs in West Africa*, entitled 'Mary Kingsley', in which he said:

'Few women are able as Mary Kingsley was able, to draw forth by the magic of her earnest personality, the best of a man. The least of those to whom she extended the privilege of her friendship were always welcome, and never failed to secure her presence ... her words of sympathy and encouragement were a fresh incentive to push onward ... fortified against disappointment. The truest, kindest, staunchest friend that ever breathed, such was Mary Kingsley.'

John Holt had similar feelings about her and expressed them in his direct and simple way in a letter he wrote to Morel ten years after her death.

'Just look what Mary Kingsley did for us all. She gave us credit for having some kind of human charity in our hearts, of having some good in us, and what endless trouble she gave herself to bring it out of us. Look at her incessant correspondence with all kinds of people in order to bring out the good that was lying dormant in their hearts, and to make use of it for other people's benefit. Think of De Cardi; of Hudson, of

Eight Years of Achievement

myself, and of Batty, and many others with whom she corresponded. I should never have taken the interest in African affairs that I have done, except for Mary Kingsley; her writings to me compelled me to think, and made me think of things away from self altogether.' [3]

These passages throw light on Mary's ways of 'working through a man'. John Holt continued till his death in 1915 to fight for honourable and humane treatment for the African peoples, and had a decisive influence in checking the spread of the diplomatic bargaining away of African territory and its people's liberties in the form of concessions to foreign governments, a process which Mary had so much deplored.[4]

Another side to the picture—and a more sombre one—is Mary's own reactions to other people. The plain truth seems to be that she did not generally like people very much—she preferred mango swamps and the Erdgeist; she was shy and critical in an English drawing-room. She could not bring her bushman nature into harmony with the disingenuous features of social life. She did not enjoy being lionized. Writing to Lady Macdonald a year after her return, she says:

'I was yesterday at two At Homes and a dinner, at every one of which I saw people who had abused their hosts up hill and down dale or who their hosts had abused ditto. Yet there they all were together smiling and calling each other by their Christian names and so on—it all seems to me silly and sinful and it's uncommon dull.' [5]

To Hatty Johnson in Cambridge she wrote of a week of academic visits, 'The whole week has been too full of intellectual society for my weak brain as I am about as repaying from a social point of view as a chrysalis.' In another letter to the same friend she describes a very revealing encounter with some of her fellows.

'I was at the writers' club yesterday and was an utter failure

Books and Friends

—because I was frightened by a little woman about 4 feet 6 inches high who had been to Kimberley. It wasn't that that terrified me but her shirt and fixings, real shirt, starched, studs, waistcoat and coat and hat on side of head, talked of how women should let people see they could *boss* it. I shrunk into a corner with a little lady who had really been to the Faroe Islands and who could have wiped up the other one, shirt and all, in fact the whole room full, only she did not know it and told me lots of things, and above all she did not know who I was and asked me if I was related to Tinsley the publisher, I said I thought I might be.' [6]

'The majority of people I meet I shrink from', Mary wrote. In a letter to the same friend her brother Charles expresses similar sentiments. Both had of course suffered from their early environment, and Charles seems to have been rather a waif, though he was a cultured man, and had some devoted friends. But Mary's shrinking from people did not prevent her from understanding them, or from acquiring an enormous circle who were proud to call themselves her friends.

Among those who did not frighten her were the Kiplings. She had a great admiration for Kipling's works and was glad to make his acquaintance. Mrs Kipling found her a 'delightful woman'. Kipling expressed the view that she was beyond frightening. He said, 'Being human she must have been afraid of something, but one never found out what it was.' [7]

He was not intimate enough with Mary to know what frightened her most, for it related to her deepest feelings and affections. Her experiences as a child and young woman had filled her with the fear of death—other people's to be sure, not her own; and of illness. In these later years she was constantly anxious about her brother, whose health was very delicate. Among those whom she did not like were most of her Kingsley relatives, as letters to Miss Johnson reveal; but to her brother

Eight Years of Achievement

she was wholly devoted and in the midst of her innumerable commitments caring for Charley came always first. In January 1897 she wrote to Miss Johnson, 'I am going to absolutely loathe being in England. I could bear it if Charley enjoyed himself, but he don't; do what I can with my small means to make things comfortable for him.'

Five months later she speaks again of her anxiety:

'I feel the fear coming down on me that there is something wrong with his lungs, and I feel so powerless in the matter. It is just as if the old days were coming back and I do not feel able to work, or think on outside things as I could were it not for this.'

Her correspondence with Sir Alfred Lyall was mainly on anthropological matters, but now and then there is a very personal note. She was fond of Lady Lyall, and in a letter of May 1898 speaks of the fear of wearying her by calling too often: 'But she is so restful and pleasant to me whose home is in the valley of the shadow of death. I thought when I left Cambridge that I had left that valley, but it was an error.'

When she wrote this she was deeply under the shadow owing to the recent death of the dearest of her friends, Lady Goldie.

There was in Mary's own nature much feminine gentleness but the hard school of her childhood in a home alternately deprived and tempestuous had driven these qualities into hiding. She valued them all the more in her women friends—in Lady Lyall, in Lady Macdonald, and above all in Lady Goldie, whom she deeply loved and 'who loved me'. Lady Goldie died in April 1898. Mary wrote to Mr Kemp:

'From the first time I saw her she fascinated me, and has exercised an immense influence over me, that I feel lost without her. In all this West Coast battle of politics and factions with their unfair abuse of each other's intentions she was so apart from all that was evil in it, so loving to all that was

Books and Friends

good, that people used to think she did not understand. I only wish I understood one tenth part as well.' [8]

And to John Holt:

'Lady Goldie's death is the reason of my distracted silence. I was very fond of her. She was a sweet gentle woman so unlike the majority of these fashionable smart foolish folk here who bore, weary and disgust me with their ignorance, conceit and airs of grandly good intentions. I feel I have lost something I can never have replaced. I can do my own devilry, and sneer and gibe, and when it's necessary think, but I do them all savagely: I hate to see natives killed and England's honour to them broken. I hate to see a noble set of Englishmen held cheap and libelled; she never hated anything.' [9]

The depth of Mary's sorrow over this friend's death is revealed in the strange dedication of *West African Studies*. 'To my brother, Mr C. G. Kingsley, and to my friend who is dead.'

Another dear friend, herself a fighter and reformer, was Mrs J. R. Green, the wife of the historian. Mrs Green was devoted to Mary and did her best to take care of her. She was rewarded by an almost clinging affection. 'I must have you and Goldie,' Mary wrote to her, 'I must be allowed to warm myself at your hearth-stones.' And again: 'I should be miserable without you.'

To her different friends and correspondents she showed very different aspects of her character. It was to two men that she seems to have written most intimately of her deepest thoughts and feelings—the missionary Mr Kemp, and a friend of her last two years, Sir Matthew Nathan. Writing to Mr Kemp in 1898 she said:

'It is a sad situation for you, a Wesleyan, to be father confessor to what is honestly and truly a very tortured soul. As for my not showing the best part of me—well, the best part

Eight Years of Achievement

of me is all this doubt, and self-distrust and melancholy, and heartache over other people. Why should I show it to people I don't care for and don't know? I put on armour and coruscating wit, according to Stead—who is too big a fool to see through it—when I go out to battle. If I did not—well, I should be like Goldie, hurt and embittered, and in my case, *not* in his, unfit for combat.' [10]

Though her agnostic upbringing had deprived her of what are called the consolations of faith, she was too wise to think she could acquire faith by the unaided intellect. In an earlier letter to Mr Kemp she said:

'Please do not think I admire, or for the matter of that, that any of the scientific tribe I was brought up amongst, admire what is called broad-minded theology. We don't, we despise the person who tries to reconcile religion and science, by twisting both of them out of shape and meaning.'

Mary had herself no tendency to be either orthodox or atheistical. In a letter to Sir Alfred Lyall she tells of being distressed about a friend who was trying to console herself for a bereavement through the aid of spiritualists, and comments: 'Oh, dear, why will people who don't *believe* in God let go the end of the string of orthodoxy? I can let go safely because I *do*.'

Mary met Sir Matthew Nathan, then Major Nathan, in February 1899 and was greatly attracted to him; partly because he was a Jew, and she liked Jews, ('Their attraction for me is their dreamy minds, their hard common sense and their love for beautiful material objects') and also because he was taking up the onerous post of administering Sierra Leone, a colony still in a very rebellious state. Mary admired Nathan's courage, and was deeply concerned for his success and welfare. In the few remaining months of her life she wrote some very revealing letters to him; one of them in which she describes herself

Books and Friends

as a 'gust of wind' has been quoted earlier in this biography. Nathan seems to have been at first a little afraid that Mary's reforming zeal and great influence among the Africans might increase his difficulties in the colony. The Colonial Office were certainly uneasy about her power over both white traders and educated Africans. She writes to assure him that although she has 'the entire confidence of the educated "nig" throughout West Africa' . . . she does 'not want this power thing at all'—she continues to hate and distrust the hut tax, but she will do nothing, she assures him, to make the task of British officers forced to collect the tax any more difficult than it was bound to be. But as far as the principle involved went, she could not just 'lie by silent and save people's feelings, things it hurts me to hurt'. There are a few people, she then tells Nathan, and he is one of them, whose good opinion she needs to have if her life is to seem worth living. She ends this letter by saying that she had been meeting relations of his, who were anxious for his safety. 'They gave me a criminal feeling of responsibility for the climate. Allah send it treats you well. It would if I had power. . . . Remember as kindly as you can that melancholy thing that will always serve and fear you, M. H. Kingsley.' [11]

How far Nathan responded to this impulsive and confiding friendship is not clear. His letters to her have presumably disappeared with her other papers. According to Mrs Green he showed respect for her only while she was useful to him, and after her death was as indifferent to her memory as to her ideals. We know that her last meetings with him, when he was back in England early in 1900, were disturbed by disagreements. She wrote to Mr Holt: 'I see a good deal of Nathan and quarrel with him, for he is one of those who see nothing for it but the hut tax.' And to Stephen Gwynn:

'I have had a most distressing row with Nathan which grieves me—but still it was comic; there was he the Jew and

Eight Years of Achievement

I the Dane, both equally feeling we were English to the Backbone and right in our divergent views—both of us unlike the great mass of English as we, or they, are to Chinese.'

(It seems to have been a whim of Mary's to refer to herself often as a Dane and sometimes as an Irishman.)

Her letter to Gwynn ends with these words: 'I am going out early in March.' She was going out, not to her beloved Coast, but to see if she could help her country in South Africa. Soon after the Boer War started she had felt it her duty to offer her services; but as the months went on and it appeared she was not needed, her hopes had risen of going back to the Coast. On 14 February 1900 in a letter to Mr Holt she says:

'I am very depressed and worried, for some months ago I volunteered to go out to South Africa in connection with nursing work, was told I was not wanted and it would all be over in no time, last week I was told I was wanted, and I expect to start the first or second week in next month.'

She seems to have foreseen what was in store for her. In her last lecture given at the Imperial Institute on 12 February, she spoke of the kindness of audiences in listening to her discourses on West Africa, and said: 'I humbly beg to thank you all most sincerely on this, the last night I shall, in all human probability, have the honour of speaking to London,' and she ended her lecture with the sailor's refrain: 'Goodbye and fare you well', adding, 'for I am homeward bound.'

The journey home was short, but hard.

9

The Last Job

In September of 1899 Mary had been fully intending to go again to the Coast. Sir George Goldie wrote to her:

'*I am more grieved than I can say* to hear you are going to West Africa again—not that I fear for your health (so much); you have proved your power of resistance to the climate; but because your friends at home will miss you sadly. Moreover your *own* work—that of which you write—will stand still while you are away. How can you teach Demos from the swamp and bush of Africa?' [1]

Poor Mary! She had worked very hard teaching Demos; she wanted now to go and play: to watch the tropical moonlight on lonely lakes; to shoot rapids in a canoe; to pilot small steamers over sandbars; to meet, to laugh with, to manage those untamed Africans who, she said, understood her so much better than the inhabitants of English drawing-rooms. But her friends at home did not appear to recognize the call of the wild. Her conscience and fate intervened; she took on a job far more exacting and distressing, and as it proved more dangerous for her, than any she had had before.

On the voyage out to the Cape she managed to write several long letters to friends as well as the letter for the journal, *The New Africa*, quoted in Chapter VI. Conditions, even for writing

Eight Years of Achievement

letters—even for Mary to write letters—were not easy. She wrote to Strachey on 22 March 1900, from the '*Moor*', describing the pandemonium on board—with bands, gramophone, and 650 soldiers, all uncomfortably muffled up in unsuitably warm clothes, and spending part of their time practising firing at the sea in order to learn how to handle their guns. Many soldiers were seasick, or sun-struck, or made ill by inoculations, and Mary herself had a kind of mild scarlet-fever. She amused herself by writing an article on a seventeenth-century slave-trader, Thomas Phillips, who with his crew and cargo had a still more uncomfortable time of it. The article appears as an appendix in the second (and posthumous) edition of *West African Studies*.

At Cape Town Mary found the Kiplings, who were very glad to see her. Rudyard's admiration for her was increased by her unselfish desire to be useful at the Base Camp.[2] She lost no time in reporting to medical Headquarters. She was asked by the Officer in Command if she would be willing to go to the prisoners' hospital at Simonstown to nurse Boers, 'evidently expecting that I wouldn't. I said "If that's what you want done, yes". It was. Those prisoners were dying in a way British authorities did not approve of.'

In a long letter to St Loe Strachey in May she sent a detailed account of the conditions she had to deal with. It was important for the Editor of the *Spectator* to know the truth, especially as public concern was growing in Britain over the death rate from enteric fever among the prisoners. The fever had started as a result of shocking conditions in the first camps, and had, as Mary told Mrs Green, broken out 'just when science could have told the authorities that it would; but science, as I have said before, is not attended to, so the authorities were unprepared'. The Palace Barracks were converted into a hospital without being even whitewashed, 'or in any way made suitable for the purpose; into it they sent the wretched

The Last Job

patients, and gave it to an already over-worked doctor to see after, omitting to supply either nurses or proper orderlies'.

At this date Florence Nightingale had still ten years to live, but they were ten years of dimmed intelligence, and she may have known little of the disregard of her teaching shown in this, the first British war since the Crimea.

Once the authorities woke up to the situation, so Mary told Strachey, absolutely no expense was spared to save the prisoners. There was an unlimited supply of brandy, milk, eggs, champagne, but there was a 'shortage of people to see the prisoners got the aforesaid. The affair has suffered from the usual lack of organizing power, absence of mobility, and the curse of clerking—write, write, write, report, examine, but to get off paper and down on facts is evidently extremely difficult in this country.'[3]

When she arrived in the hospital there were two nurses, working night and day, but unable to do more than feed the patients and see that they at least died in their beds, as most of them were delirious. Then Mary went in, and thirty new patients were sent down. It was terrible work:

'With my usual luck', she exclaimed, 'I have dropped in for a repulsive job. . . . The medical officers have moved heaven and earth to improve matters, and now I think I may say it has been done and things will go better; but I never struck such a rocky bit of the Valley of the Shadow of Death in all my days as the Palace Hospital, Simonstown.'

She was by now well qualified as a nurse, and had considerable medical knowledge. Besides the long experience she had acquired in her own home she had always felt it her duty to help in nursing the sick, going to the aid of relatives and friends in England, and of such black or white men as she was allowed to help when on her travels. One of her quarrels with mission personnel in West Africa she told Mr Holt in one of

Eight Years of Achievement

her letters, was due to their stubborn adherence to the conventions even in matters of life and death.

'I have never forgiven one of the best of the white women saying to me when I said I was going down that night to nurse a sick man, white, that was ill unto death with fever that had been neglected for days, with none other white Christian close by while I was away, that "Miss Kingsley you cannot, it's not respectable". Of course I went.' [4]

No questions of the conventions could arise in the Palace Hospital. Strong rough men in violent delirium had to be chased down the wards and hauled back to their beds, only too often to die there. The stench was 'unutterable', and bugs and lice were in plentiful supply. Under these circumstances the chances of contracting the fever were intensified, as Mary well knew. And this time she did not want to die—not then, and not in that place. It was a very different matter to court death in the jungles and fever swamps of West Africa. One of the nurses who was working with Mary afterwards reported that she had taken to smoking and drinking wine instead of water in the hope of staving off infection.

She wrote an account to Mrs Green of the awful conditions with which she was trying to deal, and ended her letter with what was obviously intended as a possible last farewell:

'I am down in the ruck of life again. Whether I shall come up out of this, like I came up out of what is associated with thinking proper, I don't know.* It is a desperate game I am playing here, and it is doubtful. One nurse and an orderly

---

* Mary uses the word 'thinking' here and often in a curious sense—as meaning scientific investigation such as she pursued on her West African expeditions. She felt hard clear thinking to be a duty, and could never, she tells Mrs Green in a letter, accept any conclusion without first fighting against it. 'Therefore I am in a continual state of thinking hard, which is very uncomfortable. It is evidently much easier to feel one's way through life.' (Feb. 12, '97.)

Fishing canoe and beach, near Victoria

The Last Job

who have only been on two days are down themselves. But if I do not, believe me, my dear lady, I am eternally grateful to you for all your tenderness, your infinite toleration and thoughtfulness for me. I who was and am and never shall be anything but a muddler. All this work here, the stench, the washing, the enemas, the bed pans, the blood, is my world. Not London society, politics, that gateway into which I so strangely wandered—into which I don't care a hairpin if I never wander again. Take care of yourself. You can do so much more than I in what Strachey calls *Haute Politique*, and remember it is this *Haute Politique* that makes me have to catch large powerful family men by the tails of their nightshirts at midnight, stand over them when they are sinking, tie up their jaws when they are dead. Five and six jaws a night have I had of late to tie up. DAMN the *Haute Politique*.' [5]

From some passages in her letters to Strachey one wonders that she did not add 'DAMN Imperialism'. In spite of her often expressed admiration for the fighting spirit, she did in fact detest bloodshed, and she had, as we know, the deepest interest in the individuality of nations and the variety of their cultures, a variety which the commercialized nationalism of today does so little to preserve. It must have cost her something in mental struggle to hold to her faith in British Imperialism out there in the Cape among the dying Boer prisoners. She did hold to it, because she believed that British rule offered the best hope of a wise system for civilizing the continent of Africa, and for bringing science to combat its diseases and malnutrition. Yet there was a narrowness in her imperialist vision, for deeply though she felt the tragedy of the war, she does not seem to have envisaged any liberal solution such as was ultimately found. She wrote to Strachey:

'There is not an atom of doubt with whom in this fight the sympathies of the majority of the inhabitants of this colony

Eight Years of Achievement

are—namely with the Boers. The English Colonists are holding meetings everywhere in favour of complete annexation ... they know their existence as a free people depends on this being done; but the majority of the people here are not English. They don't hold public meetings; they know it is not safe for them to do so, but they think the more. ... You have got to choose whether you will have free Englishmen here or free Boers. I say we must have free Englishmen because of the Imperio-geographical positions of the place, but I am perfectly certain that that means enslaving these Boers. Your freedom of institutions, etc. etc. etc., is slavery to them, and they will not be grateful for your advantages.'

This is the hard political shell of Mary's expressed opinions. But there was a great conflict going on underneath, where her heart-ache for suffering, her own tortured and doubting spirit, her endless pursuit of facts to illumine the truth, must at this time have been more than usually tormenting. Some months before she left for Cape Town it had been, Gwynn says, less plain to Strachey than to himself, how uneasy she was about the situation. While she longed to see the right kind of British Imperialism show its strength as it had often done in the past, with benefit to all concerned, she was so well aware of the muddle, the lack of science, medical and ethnological, and worst of all the too frequent failure of a proper sense of justice, in the methods of government at that date. She had written to Gwynn some months earlier:

'If our rule were what it might be but is *not*—if it were Liberty, Justice, Representation—we *should* have the right, the divine right, to enforce it, but so long as it isn't we have *not*, we are taking unto ourselves the right of God when we are an idol.'

In a second letter, in February 1900, she wrote:

'I am deeply grieved and worried about the thing as it is.

The Last Job

My own creed in the matter is so narrow, and so hard, so much lower in some points, so much higher in others. I love my own country. I have seen for years it must go smash if it sticks to the creed it had, say this day six months back, but do anything to save the crash I felt I could not. One half of the people would shrink back in horror from half the things I would do, the other half say, "That's too fine a feeling of honour for practical politics." '

As she struggled on for those two months in the hospital, immersed in the feminine work of sick nursing, her feelings were deeply moved by the plight of the unhappy Boers. And having told Strachey what it seemed to her necessary to do in the end in support of British Imperialism, she goes on to tell him something of the price in human suffering.

'They want their own country, their very own; it works out in all their delirium—"ons Land, ons Land!" One of them held forth to me today, a sane one, how he knew every hill's name, every bend of the river's name, every twist in the road—his hills, roads, rivers, not England's, or Germany's, but "ons Land".... It is a rocky problem for the future.'

This letter was written in May. A few weeks later she suddenly sickened with enteric. One of the nurses who worked under her, and who had recently come out from England, told Stephen Gwynn afterwards that Mary had been 'the one bright spot for us, always with some amusing tale when we were at our lowest ebb'. When she fell ill she maintained at first that it was only a touch of West Coast fever, such as she had often had. When forced to admit to severe pain and fever, she refused to see any doctor but Dr Carré with whom she had worked from the start, and he was not available for a day. When he saw her she had already a perforation of the bowel, and he decided to operate at once, but it was too late to save her. When she knew that she was dying she asked the nurses

Eight Years of Achievement

to leave her alone, saying she did not want anyone to see her in her weakness. Animals, she said, went away to die alone, and she felt like them. 'It was hard', Nurse Rae said, 'for us to do this, but we left the door ajar, and when we saw she was beyond knowledge went to her.'

On 3 June 1900 her brother had a message from the War Office to say that she was dangerously ill, and he prepared to start at once for the Cape, but news of her death arrived before he could sail. On 6 June Dr Carré wrote an account of her last days to Mr A. L. Jones, the Liverpool shipowner. Mary had often mentioned her Liverpool friends in conversation with Dr Carré, and at the last had asked that she should be buried at sea, and if this could not be done in South Africa, she wished her body embalmed and sent to Mr Jones to be buried in British waters. Dr Carré wrote:

'Knowing thus of Miss Kingsley's friendship with you I take the liberty of sending this note containing a few details of her illness and death.

'What a valuable life thrown away, poor Miss Kingsley! No one but myself can know what work she did here and what confidence and trust she put in me. I must often have been wrong in my ideas, I must often in the stress of overwork have been most irritable, and yet never once did Miss Kingsley question the wisdom of my orders or actions; all she did was to obey and ever express her wish to do "anything" which would help me. And she did help me through one of the most difficult tasks I could have been given to do; without that help I could never have done here what has been done, and what credit *I* get for the success of the work here in great measure belongs to *her*. I was sent to Simonstown to combat the crisis created by the outbreak of enteric fever among the Boer prisoners of war, and after I had been here about a week Miss Kingsley joined me in the capacity of a "Nursing Sister" and

The Last Job

between us in an incredibly short time we converted chaos into order, or as she herself has written it, converted "a mortuary into a sanatorium".

'Unfortunately as events have shown she greatly overtaxed her strength, and this wretched war claims yet another brilliant victim, a thoroughly good woman of giant intellect whom this world can ill spare. . . . I shall always recall Miss Kingsley's memory as one of the saddest and greatest friendships of my life.

'It will be a great satisfaction to her brother and her friends to know that though only two months in Simonstown she had won the love and respect of all, and her funeral at sea, in accordance with her most definitely expressed wishes, was I suppose the most imposing obsequies this small place has ever witnessed.' [6]

The many obituary articles and letters which appeared in English papers in the weeks following Mary's death reveal almost as much depth of affection for her as a person, as admiration for her mind and work. We can see from these how strong an impression she had made on her contemporaries. Notices deploring her death appeared also in many Continental papers. One of the longest notices appeared on 16 June 1900 in the *Athenaeum*, and is signed merely 'Gamma'. Mary had at least four close friends whose surnames began with G: Green, Gwynn, Günther and Goldie; from the context of this notice Sir George Goldie seems the most likely writer. The notice opens with these words:

'It is difficult in speaking of the premature death of Miss Mary Kingsley not to use language which to those who did not know her, or only knew her as it were, from the outside, may seem to savour of exaggeration. To those, on the other hand, who knew her as she was, with all the variety of her richly endowed nature, her commanding intellect, her keen insight, her originality, her tenderness, her simplicity, her absolute

Eight Years of Achievement

freedom from cant or pretence, her delightful humour, her extraordinary grasp of the problems, physical, ethnological, or political, to which as occasion arose she turned her attention, any attempt to portray her character or to estimate by how much the world is the poorer for her loss must fall short of the reality.

'It is barely four years since the daughter of Dr George Kingsley, the niece of Charles and Henry Kingsley, became suddenly famous on her return from the second West African journey. And yet so full of intense and varied and beneficent activity has her life been since, so much has she impressed her countrymen by her writings and her lectures, so rapidly has she won the admiration and affection of an ever-increasing circle of friends, that it is impossible in this place to do more than touch briefly upon her main achievements and her claim to lasting remembrance.

'Something of her early training and experiences may be gathered from the admirable memoir which she recently prefixed to the collected volume of her father's *Notes on Sport and Travel*. Indeed, much that she tells us of her father might literally be transferred to herself. Thus, "his fearless brilliant grey eyes looked right into the hearts of those who spoke with him"; "his conversation, ranging easily through every subject from philosophy to fishing, full of dry humour and flashing with brilliant wit and trenchant repartee, had a charm which was absolutely irresistible"; "he knew books only less well than he knew men, men only less well than he knew nature". Do not these phrases vividly recall the noble, gifted woman who wrote them only a few months ago, and has now fallen a victim to her insatiable desire to help her fellow creatures, of whatever race and colour, in their distress?'

The notice concludes:

'Her death is the fitting crown of a life of noble self-sacrifice,

The Last Job

but it may be doubted whether any life so valuable has been lost to the nation since the war began. What her loss means to her friends can only be expressed by the one word, irreparable.'

Her death was lamented by her friends among the merchants. A prominent business man wrote to Mrs Green: 'We in the African Trade have lost a true friend, one who knew our weak points and who boldly gave us credit for our good ones. She knew all about us and our affairs and got at facts in a most marvellous way. . . . I could have given my business over to her.' [7]

In June 1901, reviewing the second edition of *West African Studies*, Morel wrote: 'It was written on the book of Fate that she should die just as the practical usefulness of her work, its high morality and extreme accuracy, were forcing themselves upon the notice of her contemporaries in politics, administration and commerce, and upon the imagination of thinking England. . . . Those who knew her, and believed in her knowledge and capacity, are asking themselves today whether she died too soon for her counsels to have made any but a fleeting impression upon the minds of men, or whether they have taken root and are destined to bring forth fruit.' Morel looked, he said, to the newly formed African Society to spread the ideas which Mary had taught.[8]

The African Society was founded as a national memorial to Mary Kingsley within a few months of her death. It owed its foundation very largely to the initiative of John Holt, A. L. Jones and Mrs Green. It continues to this day as the Royal African Society and Article I of its constitution states that it has been created to commemorate Mary Kingsley's work, and to investigate further the institutions, religion and history of the African races and to secure their welfare. Every number of its Journal has on its title page a small portrait medallion of

Eight Years of Achievement

Mary's head. Proposals were also made for starting in Liverpool a hospital for the study of tropical diseases.*

The inaugural meeting of the Society was held on 27 June 1901. Among its numerous members and patrons it included the distinguished names of Lord Avebury, Viscount Cromer, J. G. Frazer, Sir Harry Johnston, Lord Lugard, Sir Alfred Lyall, and Mrs Humphrey Ward.

There is no doubt that Mary Kingsley's influence penetrated into the whole texture of thinking on colonial problems, and that her sympathy for the African peoples did much to dispel the hostile and contemptuous attitude that had so often been manifested towards them by white races. Many years after her death a writer on the customs of the Ashanti, Captain Rattray, wrote to Stephen Gwynn:

'Miss Kingsley was the greatest white woman who ever went to West Africa, and proud I am to have had my efforts coupled with such a name.

'In some ways I think she was inspired. Her face (I only know it from an old photograph in an old poke bonnet) has always struck me as a beautiful face. I would willingly have given a few years of life to have met her.'

Perhaps the finest tribute to her influence was paid by a French writer on colonialism, M. Emile Baillaud. In his studies of English colonial history he refers constantly to Mary's teaching. Gwynn quotes several passages translated from this writer, among them the following:

'The distance traversed in the years between 1890 and 1900 by both France and England in regard to West Africa is difficult to realize. In France it was the explorers who made an end of the public's indifference. But it was left almost entirely

* It was not found possible to establish a hospital, but a Mary Kingsley Medal for research into tropical diseases was instituted at the Liverpool School of Tropical Medicine.

The Last Job

for Mary Kingsley, single-handed, to fix the attention of England on the work that had to be done in West Africa and to indicate the methods that must be employed to accomplish it. . . .

'When she made her first African journey, nobody had yet thought of asking whether the line of action adopted by white men was the best suited to ensure a rational development of their relations with the natives, or what were the principles on which this line of action should be based. . . . To grasp these principles, and to gain acceptance for them, it was necessary to change the indifference or contempt displayed by almost all who till then had been in contact with the blacks, for that profound love which in Mary Kingsley extended itself to all mankind.

'But the wonderful thing about her was the alliance of this power of divination and sympathy to a perfect understanding of the needs of the countries she studied. And so, though men of her race had been coming to Africa for years, they had to wait for a woman to show them by labour such as no other woman had conceived and carried out, the things that they had never been able to see.'

That the nursing sister who had died in a small military hospital in South Africa was a pioneer to whom her country owed much, was acknowledged by the military and naval honours, the torpedo-boat, the firing party, the muffled drums, which attended her funeral at sea—honours never before shown to a woman.

Mary was in her thirty-eighth year when she died and she had had only eight years in which to use freely her great abilities and express her extraordinary vitality. She had not wasted her time. But her political work and teaching, though it had absorbed most of her energies, was only a part of the legacy which she has left to future generations. She has left an

Eight Years of Achievement

inspiring story of fearless adventure in pursuit of 'the inner knowledge of God', and of closer communion with the Erdgeist, the all-consoling; and records of a personality admirable for its integrity, memorable and lovable for its oddity and variety—its tenderness and ferocity, its laughter and pity.

Notes and References

Note on the Portraits

Frontispiece: This hitherto unpublished portrait is reproduced by kind permission of Mr C. R. Holt. It was sent to John Holt by Mary Kingsley's brother Charles with this comment: 'The enlarged photograph which I promised Mrs Holt was not a success. But I found a very pretty full-length portrait of my sister a short time ago. It must have been taken, I fancy, just after her return from her second journey to the W. Coast when I was abroad for I have never seen it before. I will send you a copy of this in a day or two's time.'

The portrait opposite p. 144 is the one reproduced in Gwynn's *Life* and in *West African Studies*. One assumes these photographs are of the same date—since the hat and other clothes are identical—but perhaps, in Mary's case, the assumption is rash.

One other portrait, which I do not give, is published by Gwynn. It shows Mary side-face in a black toque. Gwynn describes it as 'from an old newspaper illustration'. It was in fact taken by the Cambridge amateur photographer, Dew Smith, and appears in Edward Clodd's *Memories*, 'by kind permission of Mrs Roy-Batty'.

Chapter References

CHAPTER I

1. From a letter to Sir Matthew Nathan, March 1899, quoted by Gwynn, p. 26.
2. Lecture to the Imperial Institute, 12 Feb. 1900, reprinted in second edition of *West African Studies*.
3. Memoir of George Kingsley by Mary Kingsley; see volume *Notes on Sport and Travel* by George H. Kingsley, p. 1.
4. ibid. p. 3.
5. ibid. p. 6.

Notes and References

6. Memoir of George Kingsley by Mary Kingsley; see volume *Notes on Sport and Travel* by George H. Kingsley, p. 27.
7. ibid. p. 204.
8. ibid. p. 202.
9. Letter to George Macmillan, quoted by Gwynn, p. 15. (Letters to Macmillan will in every case be quoted from Gwynn, as the originals have not been available.)
10. Memoir of G.H.K. p. 195.
11. Extracts from *Mainly about People* are taken from Gwynn. I have been unable to find a copy of the original periodical.
12. This information comes from private sources. After Professor Roy's death Mrs Roy married in 1901 the Mr Batty who had befriended Mary on her first journey and whom she had reckoned among her most intimate friends.
13. Letter to the Rev. Denis Kemp, quoted by Gwynn, p. 152.

CHAPTER 2

1. Letter to Sir Matthew Nathan, quoted by Gwynn, p. 26.
2. Holt papers.
3. *Travels in West Africa*, p. 9.
4. See Introductory Notice to 2nd edition of *West African Studies*.
5. Letter to Sir Matthew Nathan, Gwynn, p. 26.
6. T.W.A. p. 3.
7. T.W.A. p. 5.
8. T.W.A. p. 70.
9. Lecture to Cheltenham Ladies' College; see the College magazine for Autumn 1898.
10. Letter to Sir Matthew Nathan, Gwynn, p. 26.
11. W.A.S. p. 31.
12. T.W.A. p. 6.
13. W.A.S. pp. 38–9.
14. W.A.S. pp. 15–17.
15. W.A.S. p. 225.

CHAPTER 3

1. Letter to George Macmillan.
2. T.W.A. p. 57.
3. Holt papers.

Notes and References

4. Letter to Mr Irvine of Liverpool, 12 Dec. 1903. A very interesting letter discussing Mary's political aims in Africa. It is given in full in the 2nd edition of Gwynn's Life.
5. *T.W.A.* pp. 92–3.
6. *W.A.S.* p. 128.
7. *T.W.A.* p. 103.
8. *T.W.A.* p. 107.
9. *T.W.A.* p. 545.
10. *T.W.A.* pp. 417–18.
11. For the account of this expedition see *T.W.A.* Chapter IX.

CHAPTER 4

1. *T.W.A.* pp. 101 following.
2. Holt papers.
3. *T.W.A.* p. 544.
4. For the Rembwé expedition see Chapters XI–XIII of *T.W.A.*
5. Letter to the *Spectator*, 28 Dec. 1895.
6. *T.W.A.* pp. 329–30.

CHAPTER 5

1. See Gwynn, p. 92.
2. *T.W.A.* p. 544.
3. *T.W.A.* Chapters XXIV–XXVII.
4. *W.A.S.* p. 150.

CHAPTER 6

1. *W.A.S.* p. 201; *T.W.A.* p. 504.
2. *T.W.A.* p. 507.
3. *T.W.A.* p. 401.
4. *W.A.S.* p. 54.
5. For this and following passages see *W.A.S.* Chapters V–VII, and *T.W.A.* p. 505.
6. Lecture to the Psychical Research Society, quoted by Gwynn, p. 195.
7. *T.W.A.* p. 403.
8. *T.W.A.* App. I, p. 660.
9. *T.W.A.* p. 205.

Notes and References

10. *W.A.S.* p. 106.
11. *W.A.S.* p. 108.
12. *W.A.S.* p. 204.
13. Letter quoted by Gwynn, 2nd edition, p. 268.
14. Letter to Miss Hatty Johnson, July 1895.
15. Letter quoted by Gwynn, p. 48.
16. Holt papers.

CHAPTER 7

1. Letter to the *Spectator*, 28 Dec. 1895.
2. Royal African Society Journal, Autumn 1915.
3. Holt papers.
4. *T.W.A.* p. 116.
5. Holt papers.
6. Holt papers.
7. Letter to Rev. Denis Kemp, quoted by Gwynn, p. 177.
8. Holt papers.
9. Letter to Sir Matthew Nathan, quoted by Gwynn, p. 227.
10. Holt papers.
11. Holt papers.
12. Holt papers.
13. Holt papers.
14. Holt papers.
15. From MS. notes of a speech, lent by the Women's Service Library.
16. Holt papers.
17. Letter to Mrs J. R. Green, Nov. 1897. Mary's letters to Mrs Green, described by Gwynn in the preface to both editions as being lost, but in a postscript to the 2nd edition discovered and quoted from, are in the National Library of Ireland. There is now a microfilm copy at the Cambridge University Library.
18. Holt papers.
19. Letter to Mr Hartland, quoted by Gwynn, p. 272.
20. Extracts given by Gwynn, p. 206.

CHAPTER 8

1. Letter to St Loe Strachey, quoted by Gwynn, p. 208.
2. Letter to Miss H. Johnson, Jan. 1897.

Notes and References

3. Holt papers.
4. See Mrs Green's address to the African Society, 1915.
5. Letter to Lady Macdonald, quoted by Gwynn, p. 130.
6. Letter to Miss H. Johnson, Jan. 1896.
7. See C. E. Carrington's *Life of Rudyard Kipling*.
8. Letter to Mr Kemp, Gwynn, p. 185.
9. Holt papers.
10. Letter to Mr Kemp, quoted by Gwynn, p. 187.
11. Letter to Sir Matthew Nathan, quoted by Gwynn, p. 220.

CHAPTER 9

1. Letter quoted by Gwynn, p. 264.
2. See C. E. Carrington's *Rudyard Kipling*.
3. For this and following letters to Strachey see Gwynn, Chapter XII.
4. Holt papers.
5. Letter to Mrs Green.
6. Holt papers.
7. Mrs Green's memorial address to the African Society, June 1901.
8. E. D. Morel, reviewing 2nd edition of *W.A.S.* in the *Speaker*, 15 June 1901.

Bibliography

There are innumerable brief mentions of Mary Kingsley in books about West Africa. I have selected for mention only those books and articles which contribute to our knowledge of her as a person.

Travels in West Africa, by Mary Kingsley. Macmillan, 1897.
West African Studies, by Mary Kingsley. Macmillan, 1899; 2nd ed. 1901.
Notes on Sport and Travel, by G. H. Kingsley (with Memoir by his daughter, Mary Kingsley). Macmillan, 1900.
The Story of West Africa, by Mary Kingsley. Horace Marshall, 1900.
Folklore of the Fjort, by R. Dennett (with Introduction by Mary Kingsley). Folklore Society, London, 1897.
Royal African Society Journal, 1901, 1907.
Affairs of West Africa, by E. D. Morel (with Foreword on Mary Kingsley). Heinemann, 1902.
Nigeria: its Peoples and its Problems, by E. D. Morel. Smith Elder, 1911.
Memories, by Edward Clodd (with chapter on Mary Kingsley). Chapman & Hall, 1916.
Garden Wisdom, by Stephen Gwynn (essay on 'A lover of Justice'). Dublin, 1921.
Pioneer Women. Third Series, by E. M. Tabor, 1930.
St Loe Strachey, his Life and his Paper, by Lucy St Loe Strachey. Gollancz, 1930.
Life of Mary Kingsley, by Stephen Gwynn. Macmillan, ed. 1, 1932; ed. 2, 1933. Penguin Books, 1940. (The text of these three editions is not identical.)
Sir George Goldie, Founder of Nigeria, by D. Wellesley and S. Gwynn. Macmillan, 1934.
British Commonwealth Leaflets: Mary Kingsley, A Memoir. H.M.S.O., 1948.
Canon Charles Kingsley, by U. Pope-Hennessey. Chatto, 1948.
Ladder of Bones, by Ellen Thorpe. Cape, 1956.
Lugard: The Years of Adventure, by Margery Perham. Collins, 1956.
This is your Home, by Kathleen Wallace. Heinemann, 1956.

Index

Africa (West Coast):
  animals, 65, 66, 76, 87, 92, 102, 103–7
  diseases, 42, 45, 58, 147
  forests, 49, 73, 82, 97, 109, 111
  insects, 51, 56, 76
  mangrove swamps, 65, 66, 114
  mists, 49, 54, 72, 109, 114
  surf, 49, 69
  tornadoes, 52, 103
African:
  cannibals (see Fans)
  characteristics and ideas:
    cheerfulness, 122, 128
    gentleness, 122
    ideas about—
      death, 124 foll.
      human sacrifice, 127
      law, 96, 129, 143
      myths, 123
      secret societies, 105
      sin, 125, 126
      spirits, 124 foll.
      witchcraft, 125, 131
    lack of history, 123, 124
    lack of skills, 88, 128
    logicality, 124
    love of clothes, 62, 78, 86, 95
    love of trade, 63, 75, 84, 85, 86, 122
    melancholy, 126, 132
    use of gesture, 121
  chiefs, 127, 143
  children, 126
  converts, 129, 130, 131, 134
  educated, 133, 148, 171

  tribes:
    Ajumba, 41, 88, 99
    Ba-Fan, 85
    Bubis, 62
    Fans, 41, 68, 73, 74, 76, 90, 101, 102
    Fjorts, 58
    Igalwas, 41, 43, 76, 88
    Kru, 55
    M'pongwe, 41, 76, 78, 99
    westernized, 54, 112, 129, 148
African Society, the, 183
Alemba rapids, 80
Athenaeum, 181

Baillaud, E., 184–5
Batanga, S.S., 62, 69
Blyden, Dr, 134, 146
Boer prisoners, 174 foll.
Boer war, 172, 173 foll.
British Colonial administration, 139 foll., 157
  Colonial office, 141 and foll., 171
  Crown Colony system, 149, 153

Calabar, 63, 65, 127, 131
Cameroons, 56, 59, 107
Cameroons Mountain, 107 and foll.
Cardew, Sir Frederick, 146, 150
Carré, Dr, 179, 180
Chalmers, Sir David, 150
Chamberlain, Joseph, 14, 144, 149, 151, 153, 157
Cheltenham Ladies' College, lecture to, 50, 83, 85
Christianity in Africa, 129, 130, 134

Index

Civilization in Africa, 131, 146
Colonization, 57, 148
Congo:
  Belgian, 56
  French, 56, 58, 68 foll.
  Portuguese, 56
Cromer, Lord, 155, 156
Ctenopoma Kingsleyae, 41, 160

Dennett, R., 58, 156
Diaries, M.K.'s, 10, 61, 74, 107, 120, 162

Ecological knowledge, 147
Economic policies, 145, 146
Efoua village, 94
Egaja village, 95
English Mechanic, The, 28

Fear, varieties of, 87
Fernando Po, 62
Fetish worship, 121, 125, 131; uses of, 148
Forests, living in, 83; seeing in, 82
Forget, M. and Mme, 75, 77
Freetown, 45, 54
French:
  Colonial policy, 58, 145, 146
  Customs, 70
  Embassy, 146

Gaboon, 69, 70, 73, 88
Gacon, M. and Mme, 75, 76
Galton, Sir Francis, 16, 18
Geography, M.K.'s knowledge of, 88, 161
Goldie, Sir George Taubman, 15, 67, 147, 149, 170, 173
Goldie, Lady, 168
Gorer, G., 122
Green, Mrs J. R., 10, 38, 154, 162, 169, 174, 176, 183
Guillemard, Dr, 41, 161, 163
Günther, Dr, 41, 156

Gwynn, Stephen, 9, 10, 121, 137, 164; letters to, 58, 171, 178

Hat, M.K.'s, 94
Haute Politique, 177
Holt, C. R., 9, 10, 187
Holt, John, 10, 48, 139, 140, 165, 166, 187; letters to, 36, 64, 84, Chap. VII *passim*, 169, 172
Honour, M.K.'s notions of, 130, 141, 179
Hudson, Mr, 70, 99
Hut tax, 143, 146, 150, 171

Ideas, travelling on, 100
Imperial Institute, lecture to, 16, 172
Imperialism, 141, 145, 178

Jacot, M. and Mme, 74, 88
Johnson, Charles, 10
Johnson, Miss H., 10, 166, 167
Jones, A. L., 142, 180, 183
Ju-ju, 125, 140, 147, 155

Kangwé, 74, 88
Karkola river, 90,
Kemp, Rev. Dennis, 30, 63, 135, 144, 168, 169, 170
Kingsley:
  Charles, 16, 17 and foll., 24
  Charles George (M.K.'s brother), 10, 18, 42, 167, 168
  George Henry, 17, 18, 20 foll., 40, 135
  Mrs George Henry (Mary Bailey), 19 and foll., 30
  Gerald, 17
  Henry, 16 foll.
  Rose, 131
Kingsley, Mary Henrietta:
  Heredity and family characteristics, 16–19; fighting spirit, 101, 149

Index

Kingsley, Mary Henrietta:—*contd.*
  Early Years: home in Highgate, 21; isolation of the family, 20, 24; father's character, 20 foll.; his long absences, 19, 21, 23; mother's delicate health, 20, 23; M.K.'s domestic duties and responsibilities, 24, 29; her lack of education, 24; scrapes and punishments, 25–6; self-education, 26–9.
  Youth: family moves to Cambridge, 29; mother's illness, 29; death of parents, 30; influence on her character of her home life, 20, 23, 24, 27, 30, 35–9.
  Travels: visit to the Canaries, 39; decision to travel to W. Africa, 40; reasons for going, 40, 41; her equipment, 42–3, 94; sails on S.S. *Lagos*, 44 foll.; information from old Coasters, 45, 47, 162; interest and skill in seamanship, 46, 80, 161; relations with traders, 47, 48, 49, 50, 58; interest in trade, 45, 84, 122; second journey to W. Africa: sails on S.S. *Batanga*, 62; at Fernando Po, 62; at Calabar, 63; visits Mary Slessor, 63; travels to Ogowé river, 68; at Talagouga, 75; meets Fans, 75; visits Ogowé Rapids, 76–80; explores wild regions between Ogowé and Rembwé, 88–101; climbs Cameroons Mountain, 107–19; returns home, 120.
  Life and work in England: rouses interest in West Africa, 120 foll.; growing reputation and influence, 139 foll., 165; lectures and articles, 120, 137 foll.; consulted by Joseph Chamberlain, 144; criticism and advice on colonial administration, 139 foll., 178; her homes at Addison Rd and St Mary Abbott's Terrace, 155; frequent illnesses, 154; anxiety about her brother, 167, 168; hard work, 153 foll.; social life, 146, 147, 155, 165, 166, 168; offers services on outbreak of South African War, 172; becomes nursing sister to Boer prisoners at Simonstown, 174; contracts enteric, 179; death, 180; burial at sea, 181, 185.
  Tributes to her work and character: 120, 134, 165, 180 foll.; National Memorial, 183; Mary Kingsley Medal, 184; reviews of her books, 157, 183.
  Characteristics: as writer and speaker—her accent, 19, 137–8; use of slang, 15, 46, 162; grammatical difficulties, 137, 160; literary power, 52, 163; irony, 149, 162, 170; 'brutality in statement', 159, 161; diffuseness, 158, 159; pathos, 149; humour, 13, 15, 38, 39, 67, 149.
  Enigmatical personality: 15, 164; love of science, 27, 147, 157; of statistics, 148; of nature, 37, 40, *passim*; of poetry, 164; religious beliefs, 30, 123, 135, 170; sense of responsibility, 20, 30, 59, 135, 169; loneliness, 36, 167, 169; melancholy, 30, 122, 169; courage, 38, 81, 91, 95, 167.
  Her appearance: 29, 137–8.
Kipling, Rudyard, 167, 174

Lagos, port, 69
Lagos, S.S., 44, 51
Lambarene, 73
Liquor traffic, 141, 143
Lugard, Lord, 146

Index

Lyall, Sir Alfred (anthropologist), 140, 168, 170
Lyall, Lady, 168

Macdonald, Sir Claude, 55, 68
Macdonald, Lady, 62, 162, 166, 168
Macmillan, George, letters to, 24, 47, 153, 161, 162, 164
'Mainly about People', 26
Manchester Guardian, 157
Manneville, Vicomte de, 146
Maps, 88, 160
Medical skill, M.K.'s, 96, 175, 180
Memoir of G. H. Kingsley, 23, 40, 182
'Mind Forest', 83, 121 foll.
Missionaries, 42, 74, 139, 176
Missions, 128, 129, 133, 153
Montagu, Sir Samuel, 146
Morel, E. D., 148, 165, 183
Mungo mah Lobeh, 107 foll.
Murray, Captain, 46, 62

Nathan, Sir Matthew, 169, 170, 171; letters to, 14, 37, 147, 171
N'covi, lake, 90, 93
New Africa, The, 133, 173
Niger, 68
N'jolé, 75, 77
Noise, 66, 124
Notes on Sport and Travel, by G. H. Kingsley, 22, 182

Obedience, spirit of, 38, 55
Ogowé river, 43, 68, 71, 76
Okana (or Okono) river, 85
Okyon, 63
Old Coasters, 45, 47, 162
Ouroungou, (or Orungo), 81, 88

Phillips, Thos., 174
'Picnics', 107
Portraits of M.K., 137, 187

Rattray, Captain, 184
Rembwé river, 88 foll.

'Rooming bundles', 99
Roy, Mrs, 30
Royal Niger Company, 15, 67, 147

St James Gazette, 157
St Loe Strachey, letters to, 159, 174, 177
St Loe Strachey, Mrs, 138, 165
St Paul de Loanda, 56
Schweitzer, Dr, 73, 126, 148
Sierra del Cristal, 79, 85
Sierra Leone, 45, 54
Simonstown, 174, 181
Slessor, Mary, 10, 63, 64, 65
South African War, 172
South Sea Bubbles, by the Earl and the Doctor, 21
Spectator, 87, 88, 138, 143, 174
Spinoza, 125, 145, 157
Story of West Africa, by Mary H. Kingsley, 153, 157, 162
Style, M.K.'s, 38, 137, 159, 162, 163

Talagouga, 75, 76
Trade, 75, 78, 84–7
Traders, white, 42, 47, 48, 133, 141, 183; black, 62, 130
Travels in West Africa, by Mary H. Kingsley, *passim*
Truth, the pursuit of, 38, 138, 158
Tylor, Professor, 106, 120, 156

Valley of the Shadow, 168, 175
'Vulgarity', 162

West African Studies, by Mary H. Kingsley, *passim*
Westminster Gazette, 157
Wild animals, M.K.'s feelings for, 22, 71, 105
Women's Suffrage, 151–3
World Women's Temperance Association, 45
Writers' Club, 166

For Product Safety Concerns and Information please contact our EU representative GPSR@taylorandfrancis.com
Taylor & Francis Verlag GmbH, Kaufingerstraße 24, 80331 München, Germany

www.ingramcontent.com/pod-product-compliance
Lightning Source LLC
Chambersburg PA
CBHW061445300426
44114CB00014B/1844